Family and Friends 3

Class Book

Tamzin Thompson
Naomi Simmons

OXFORD
UNIVERSITY PRESS

Scope and sequence

Words	Grammar	Phonics	Skills
1 They're from Australia!			**page 8**
Countries Seasons / Home	Present simple: *be* *Where are you from? I'm from Egypt.*	**Consonant blends:** **cr:** *crayon* **dr:** *draw, drink* **sp:** *spoon* **sn:** *snake* **pl:** *play*	**Reading:** a story: 'The Selfish Giant' **Listening:** identifying details about age, birthday, country and favourite season **Speaking:** asking and answering about age, country and favourite season **Writing:** capitalising proper nouns and sentence beginnings; writing about myself (Workbook)
2 My weekend			**page 14**
Hobbies	*like* + verb + *ing* *I like reading. I don't like fishing.* *Does he like playing chess?* *Yes, he does. / No, he doesn't.*	**Magic e:** **a_e:** *face, space* **i_e:** *kite, bike* **o_e:** *rope, stone* **u_e:** *June, cube*	**R:** a penfriends website **L:** identifying details about different penfriends **S:** choosing a penfriend based on hobbies **W:** full forms and short forms of *be* and *have*; writing an email about my hobbies (WB)
3 My things			**page 20**
My things / phrasal verbs Collections	*your / our / their* *That's their CD player.* ***Can*** for permission / requests *Can I use your computer?* *Yes, you can. / No, you can't.*	**Words with *ar*:** *car, park, shark, star, scarf*	**R:** a school project **L:** identifying details about collections **S:** talking about collections **W:** punctuation marks: question marks, commas and full stops; writing about a child's collection (WB)
Review 1			**page 26**
Extensive reading: *Family*			**page 28**
4 We're having fun at the beach!			**page 30**
Water sports Adjectives to describe places	Present continuous: affirmative and negative *I'm swimming. She isn't snorkelling.*	**all endings:** *ball, mall, wall, tall, small*	**R:** a holiday brochure **L:** identifying details about beach activities **S:** describing what you like doing on the beach **W:** spelling rules for the gerund form; writing a postcard about my trip (WB)
5 A naughty monkey!			**page 36**
Zoo animals Adjectives to describe emotions and things	Present continuous: questions and short answers *Is the crocodile eating the sandwich?* *Yes, it is. / No, it isn't.*	***or*** and ***aw*** **spellings:** **or:** *fork, horse, corn* **aw:** *straw, paw, yawn*	**R:** a story: 'The Lion and the Mouse' **L:** identifying different frames of a cartoon strip **S:** describing different frames of a cartoon strip **W:** using speech marks; writing a fact file about animals (WB)
6 Jim's day			**page 42**
Daily routine Time words	Present simple: affirmative, negative and questions *I have breakfast at eight o'clock.* *Do they live in a big house?* *Yes, they do. / No, they don't.*	***oy*** and ***oi*** **spellings:** **oy:** *boy, toy, oyster* **oi:** *coin, oil, soil*	**R:** a website about cyber school **L:** identifying details about a student's day **S:** describing daily routine **W:** proper nouns; writing information about me (WB)
Review 2			**page 48**
Extensive reading: *Animals*			**page 50**
7 Places to go!			**page 52**
Places in town Performances	Present simple and adverbs of frequency: *always, sometimes, never* *I sometimes go to the library.* Prepositions of time: *on, at, in* *My birthday is in May.*	***ow*** and ***ou*** **spellings:** **ow:** *cow, clown, flower* **ou:** *house, trousers, mouse*	**R:** a film review **L:** identifying details about free time activities **S:** describing free time activities **W:** verbs, adjectives and prepositions; writing an email to invite a friend to the cinema (WB)

1 Listen, point and repeat. 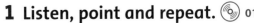 01

grandma   grandpa   mum   dad

aunt   uncle   brother   sister   cousin

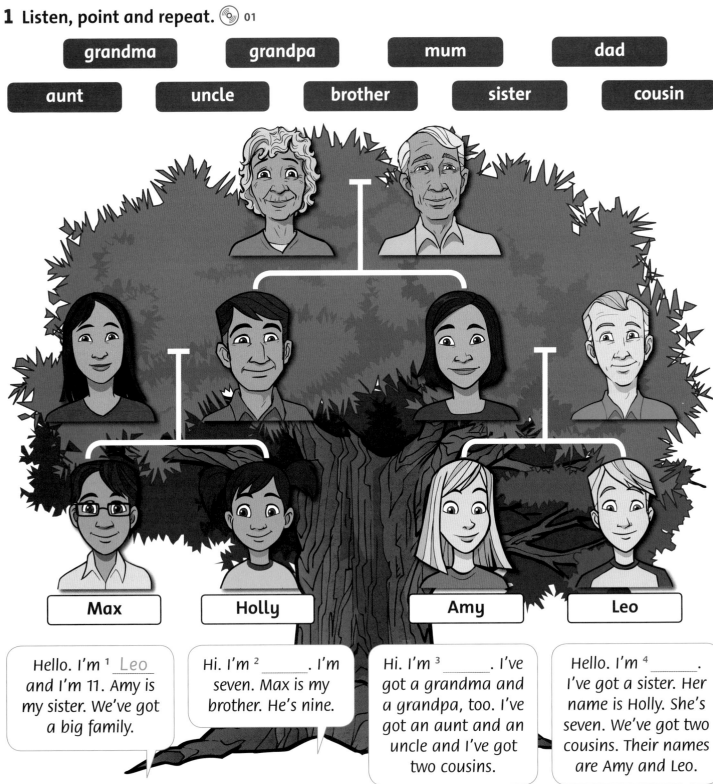

Max   Holly   Amy   Leo

Hello. I'm ¹ Leo and I'm 11. Amy is my sister. We've got a big family.

Hi. I'm ² _____. I'm seven. Max is my brother. He's nine.

Hi. I'm ³ _____. I've got a grandma and a grandpa, too. I've got an aunt and an uncle and I've got two cousins.

Hello. I'm ⁴ _____. I've got a sister. Her name is Holly. She's seven. We've got two cousins. Their names are Amy and Leo.

2 Read and write the names.

3 Listen and check. 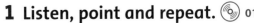 02

1 Read and write _T_ (true) or _F_ (false).

1 The red car is bigger than the blue car.   _T_
2 The green car is bigger than the blue car. ___
3 The green car is faster than the red car. ___
4 The red car is faster than the green car. ___
5 The blue car is slower than the green car. ___
6 The blue car is slower than the red car. ___

2 Write.

The elephant is _bigger_ (big) than the monkey.

The giraffe is _____ (tall) than the zebra.

The donkey is _____ (fast) than the cow.

The goat is _____ (small) than the horse.

3 Read and write _T_ (true) or _F_ (false).

1 It was sunny.   _T_
2 The children were sad. ___
3 The girl was hungry. ___
4 The boy was thirsty. ___
5 Mum and Dad were cold. ___

1 Listen and sing. 03

Twelve months in a year

January, February, March and April,
January, February, March and April,
January, February, March and April,
Twelve months in a year!

May, June, July, then August and September,
May, June, July, then August and September,
May, June, July, then August and September,
Twelve months in a year!

October, November and December,
October, November and December,
October, November and December,
Twelve months in a year!

2 Speaking Ask and answer about you.

When's your birthday?

My birthday is in June.

How old are you?

I'm nine.

1 Listen, point and repeat. 🔊 04

10 ten	20 twenty	30 thirty	40 forty	50 fifty
60 sixty	70 seventy	80 eighty	90 ninety	100 one hundred

2 Listen, point and repeat. 🔊 05

21 twenty-one

22 twenty-two

23 twenty-three

24 twenty-four

25 twenty-five

26 twenty-six

27 twenty-seven

28 twenty-eight

29 twenty-nine

3 Write the answers.

1 ten + fifty = <u>sixty</u>

2 seventy + ten = _____

3 twenty + twenty = _____

4 sixty-three + thirty-one = _____

5 thirty-two + twenty-seven = _____

6 ninety-two + eight = _____

7 forty-five + thirty-five = _____

8 ten + twenty-eight = _____

Lesson One Words

1 Listen, point and repeat. 06

Egypt

the UK

Russia

Spain

Thailand

Australia

the USA

Brazil

2 Listen and read. 07

1

Holly Where are our cousins?
Max I don't know.

2

Mum Here's a photo. That's Amy and that's Leo.
Holly Look! There they are! Hello!
Max They aren't Amy and Leo! They're from Russia. Amy and Leo are from Australia!

3

Holly Are they Amy and Leo?
Max No, they aren't. They're from the USA!
Amy Hi! Are you Max and Holly?

4

Leo I'm Leo and this is Amy. We're your cousins!
Max Really?
Amy Yes! That's an old photo!

1 Listen to the story again and repeat. Act.

2 Look and say.

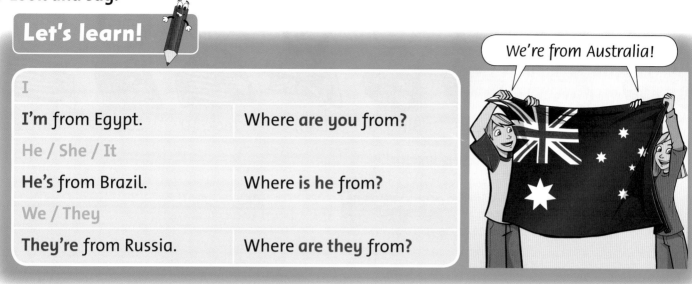

Let's learn!

I	
I'm from Egypt.	Where **are you** from?
He / She / It	
He's from Brazil.	Where **is he** from?
We / They	
They're from Russia.	Where **are they** from?

We're from Australia!

3 Read and tick (✔).

1 He's from the UK. ☐
   She's from the UK. ✔

2 They're from Brazil. ☐
   She's from Brazil. ☐

3 We're from Spain. ☐
   He's from Spain. ☐

4 They're from the USA. ☐
   I'm from the USA. ☐

4 Write. | We're She's ~~He's~~ They're |

1 Tom is nine. _He's_ from the UK.

2 Jenny is eight. _____ from Australia.

3 Anna and I are friends. _____ from Russia.

4 Jack and Carl are brothers. _____ from the USA.

1 **Speaking** Think of a boy or a girl. Ask and answer.

Jane, 8   Tom, 10   Ellie, 9   Billy, 8   Lisa, 9   Jack, 10   Zoe, 8   Carl, 8

Is it a girl?

Yes, it is.

Where is she from?

She's from the UK.

How old is she?

She's eight.

It's Jane!

2 **Write about three people.**

Jane is eight. She's from the UK. Tom is ...

3 **Listen and sing.** 08

4 **Sing and do.**

Where are you from?

Where are you from?
I'm from the UK.
Hello, hello,
How are you today?

This is my friend.
He's from the USA.
Hello, hello,
How are you today?

I'm from Brazil.
It's nice to meet you!
Hello, hello,
Nice to meet you, too.

1 Listen, point and repeat. 09

crayon   draw   spoon   snake   drink   play

2 Listen and chant. 10

We drink from a cup.
We eat with a spoon.
We draw with a crayon.
We play all afternoon.

3 Read the chant again. Circle the words from Exercise 1.

4 Circle the beginning letters. Listen and check. 11

1	2	3	4
br dr cl tr	tr cl cr sl	sm br st sp	dr sn cr pl

5	6	7	8
pr sn pl fr	sn tr dr sp	cr tr cl dr	sp cr fl pl

Reading

1 Listen, point and repeat. 🔊 12

 spring

 summer

 autumn

 winter

 garden

 season

2 Describe what's happening in the pictures below.

3 Listen and read. 🔊 13

The Selfish Giant

The giant has got a lovely garden. The children want to play in the garden, but the giant is selfish. "It's MY garden," he says. "I don't want children here." He builds a wall around the garden.

In the spring there are no flowers or birds in the giant's garden. It is winter all year. The giant isn't happy.

Then one day, the children find a hole in the wall. They go in and play. The giant hears children in his garden. There are birds and flowers, too.

The giant is happy because it is spring again. "This is your garden now, children," he says. The children are happy and the giant is not selfish now.

4 Read again and put the sentences in the correct order.

1 The giant hears children in the garden. ☐

2 The children want to play in the garden. 1

3 It is spring. But in the giant's garden it is winter. ☐

4 The giant builds a wall. ☐

5 The children and the giant are happy. ☐

6 The children find a hole in the wall. ☐

Listening

1 Listen and tick (✔). 🔊 14

1 How old is Katie?

 9 ☐  8 ✔  10 ☐

2 When is her birthday?

 April ☐   June ☐   March ☐

3 Where is she from?

 ☐  ☐   ☐

4 What is her favourite season?

 ☐   ☐  ☐

Speaking

2 Ask and answer about you.

How old are you?

I'm nine.

Where are you from?

I'm from Egypt.

What's your favourite season?

My favourite season is summer.

Writing

We use capital letters with:
countries – Spain
months – April
names – Billy

We start new sentences with capital letters.

My name is Helen.

3 Write the sentences with capital letters.

1 jenny is ten. she's from brazil.

2 i'm from spain.

3 alex is from brazil.

4 is kim from thailand?

5 it's hot in australia in december.

6 he's from egypt.

7 her birthday is in june.

My weekend

1 Listen, point and repeat. 🔊 15

read comics

skateboard

do gymnastics

play chess

fish

play basketball

take photos

play volleyball

2 Listen and read. 🔊 16

1

Amy	I've got lots of fish! Come on, Max!
Max	I don't like fishing. I like reading.
Amy	Fishing is easy. You can read your book, too.
Max	OK.

2

Max	I've got a fish!
Leo	Wow! It's a big fish!
Max	Help!

3

| Max | Take a photo, Amy! |
| Dad | That's a great fish, Max! We can have it for lunch! |

4

| Leo | It's time to go home, Max. |
| Max | Let's stay! I like fishing! |

1 Listen to the story again and repeat. Act.
2 Look and say.

Let's learn!

I / You / We / They

I **like** reading.	**Do** you **like** playing chess?
I **don't like** fishing.	Yes, I **do**. No, I **don't**.

He / She / It

He **doesn't like** skateboarding.	**Does** he **like** playing chess?
	Yes, he **does**. No, he **doesn't**.

I like fishing! Do you like fishing?

No, I don't.

3 Read and circle.

1 The girl **likes** / **doesn't like** reading comics.
2 Dad **likes** / **doesn't like** taking photos.
3 The boys **like** / **don't like** playing basketball.
4 Mum **likes** / **doesn't like** painting.

4 Write.

He _likes_ playing chess.

They _____ skateboarding.

She _____ fishing.

He _____ playing volleyball.

1 Speaking **Think of a boy. Ask and answer.**

	Alex	Lee	Fred	Max	Jack	Billy
fishing	😊	😞	😞	😊	😊	😞
skateboarding	😞	😊	😞	😞	😊	😊
basketball	😞	😞	😊	😊	😞	😊

Does he like fishing?
Yes, he does.
Does he like skateboarding?
Yes, he does.
Does he like playing basketball?
No, he doesn't.
It's Jack!

2 Write about a boy.

Lee doesn't like fishing. He likes skateboarding. He ...

3 Listen and sing. 🔘 17

4 Sing and do.

I'm happy it's the weekend!

Dad likes playing basketball,
And he likes playing chess.
Mum likes playing tennis,
But I like fishing best!

I'm happy it's the weekend,
Hip, hip, hip, hooray!
My family loves the weekend,
We have fun all day!

Mum likes drawing pictures,
And I like drawing, too.
Dad likes taking photos,
So we've got lots to do!

1 Listen, point and repeat. 🔊 18

a_e face space

Magic e makes the vowel long!

i_e kite bike

o_e rope stone

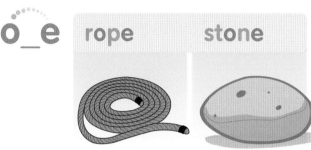

u_e June cube

2 Listen and chant. 🔊 19

Let's play together, me and you.
I've got a kite,
And a skipping rope too.

I've got a cube,
And a doll from space.
Look. It's got a purple face.

3 Read the chant again. Circle the words from Exercise 1.

4 Complete the words. Listen and check. 🔊 20

a_e   i_e   o_e   u_e

1
k _i_t_e_

2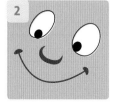
f__c__

3
st__n__

4
sp__c__

5
b__k__

6
r__p__

Skills Time!

Reading

1 Listen, point and repeat. 🔊 21

play the guitar

shop

cook

paint

play the piano

visit family

2 Look at the text. Where are the children from?

3 Listen and read. 🔊 22

www.penfriendsfromaroundtheworld.com

| Friends | **Penfriends!** | Family | Pets |

Hi! My name's Jon. I'm nine. I'm from the UK. I like playing the guitar and painting. I don't like playing chess and I really hate shopping. It's boring! What do you like doing? Email me at jon09@mailme.com!

Hello! I'm Rosa. I'm eight and I'm from Spain. I like cooking and visiting my family. I love taking photos, too. This is a photo of me and my friend. I really want a penfriend. My email address is rosa@abc.com. Please write to me!

Hi! My name's Yusuf and I'm ten. I'm Egyptian. I like playing the piano. I don't like playing volleyball but I like playing football with my friends. It's great! Do you like playing football? Send an email to me at yusuf10@quickmail.com!

4 Read again and answer the questions.

1 Does Jon like shopping? _No._

2 Does Yusuf like playing the piano? _____

3 Does Yusuf like playing volleyball? _____

4 Does Jon like playing the guitar? _____

5 Does Rosa like cooking? _____

6 Does Rosa like taking photos? _____

Listening

1 Listen and match. What do they like? 🔊 23

 1
 2
 3
 4

| Ivan | Mai | Bruno | Tina |

1 __b__
2 _____
3 _____
4 _____

a    b    c    d

Speaking

2 Ask and answer.

Billy likes ...	**Shani likes ...**	**Ting likes ...**	**Lisa likes ...**
playing volleyball	cooking	watching TV	playing the guitar
reading comics	playing tennis	playing chess	taking photos
playing basketball	painting	playing the piano	shopping

I want a penfriend.

I like taking photos.

What do you like doing?

Lisa likes taking photos.
Write an email to Lisa!

Writing

We use an apostrophe (') to make contractions.

Full form	Short form	Full form	Short form
I am	→ I'm	are not	→ aren't
she is	→ she's	I have	→ I've
it is	→ it's	it has	→ it's
we are	→ we're	has not	→ hasn't
they are	→ they're	have not	→ haven't
is not	→ isn't		

3 Write the short form.

1 Yusuf ___doesn't___ (does not) like playing volleyball.

2 Katie _____ (has not) got a brother.

3 The children are at school. _____ (They are) in the classroom.

4 We _____ (are not) hungry.

3 My things

1 Listen, point and repeat. 24

computer

TV

DVD player

CD player

MP3 player

camera

turn on

turn off

2 Listen and read. 25

1

Leo Amy, can you turn on the TV, please?
Amy Max, watch this!
Max No. I like my book.
Amy Your book is boring!
Max No, it isn't!

2

Holly Can I use your computer, Leo?
Leo Yes, you can. Have you got a school project?
Holly Yes. It's about space.

3

Holly Leo … I think it's broken.
Max My book is about space, Holly. You can read it.
Holly Well … OK.

4

Max Can I have my book, please?
Holly No! It's great!

1 Listen to the story again and repeat. Act.

2 Look and say.

Let's learn!

You	This is **your** CD.
We	That's **our** computer.
They	That's **their** CD player.

I / You / He / She / It / We / You / They

Can I **use** your computer?
Yes, you **can**.   **No**, you **can't**.

Can you **turn off** the DVD player, please?

Can I use your camera, Amy?

Yes, you can.

3 Write.   your   our   their

Is this ¹ your computer?

Yes, it's ² _____ computer.

³ _____ dog is small.
⁴ _____ dog is big.

Is this ⁵ _____ MP3 player?

No, it's ⁶ _____ MP3 player.

4 Write.

Can we turn on the television?

No, you can't.

Can he have dinner at our house?

_____

Can I use your computer?

_____

Can we listen to our CD?

_____

1 Speaking **Ask and answer.**

open the window	help me with my homework	turn on the TV
turn off the CD player	close the door	put on your coat

What's Picture 2?

Can you open the window, please?

What's Picture 6?

Can you help me with my homework, please?

2 Close your book and write three questions.

Can you open the window, please?

3 Listen and sing. 🎵 26

4 Sing and do.

It's rainy today

It's rainy today.
Can we watch a DVD?
It's rainy today.
Can we play our new CD?
It's a rainy day.
Can we watch TV?
Can you watch a show with me?
It's a rainy day.

It's sunny today.
Can we play out in the sun?
It's sunny today.
We can have a lot of fun.
Can we run and can we play?
Can you play with me all day?
It's a sunny day.

1 Listen, point and repeat. 🔊 27

ar   car   park   shark   star   scarf

2 Listen and chant. 🔊 28

We're in the car,
After playing in the park.

I've got an orange scarf,
I've got a toy shark.

3 Read the chant again. Circle the words with *ar*.

4 Match the words that rhyme. Write. | farm   star   ~~art~~   shark |

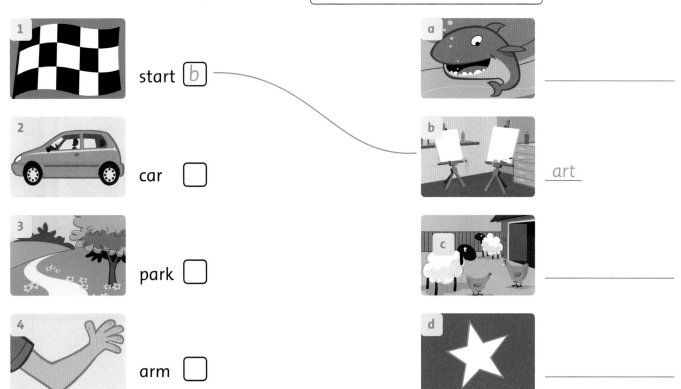

1 start [b]

2 car ☐

3 park ☐

4 arm ☐

a _____

b art

c _____

d _____

Skills Time!

Reading

1 Listen, point and repeat. 🎵 29

 **stickers**

 **posters**

 **comics**

 **postcards**

 **badges**

 **shells**

2 Describe what you can see in the pictures below.

3 Listen and read. 🎵 30

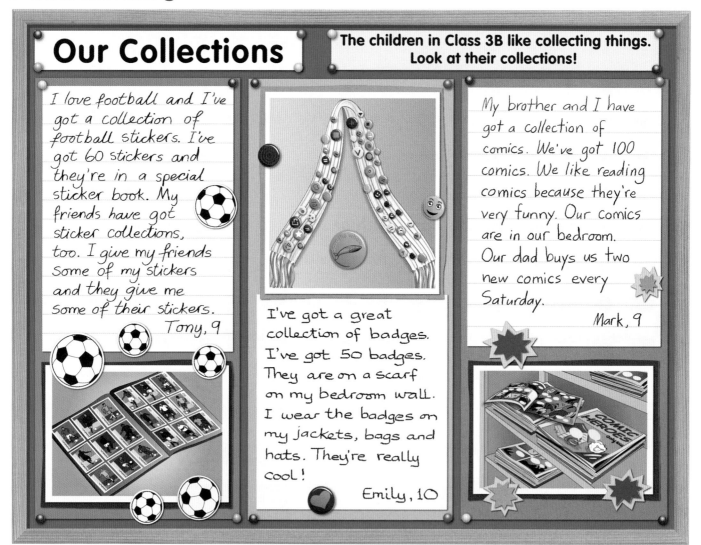

Our Collections

The children in Class 3B like collecting things. Look at their collections!

I love football and I've got a collection of football stickers. I've got 60 stickers and they're in a special sticker book. My friends have got sticker collections, too. I give my friends some of my stickers and they give me some of their stickers.

Tony, 9

I've got a great collection of badges. I've got 50 badges. They are on a scarf on my bedroom wall. I wear the badges on my jackets, bags and hats. They're really cool!

Emily, 10

My brother and I have got a collection of comics. We've got 100 comics. We like reading comics because they're very funny. Our comics are in our bedroom. Our dad buys us two new comics every Saturday.

Mark, 9

4 Read again and write.

| Mark | Emily | Tony |

1 _Tony_ loves football.

2 _____'s got a badge collection.

3 _____'s got 100 comics.

4 _____'s got 60 stickers.

5 _____ likes reading comics.

6 _____ wears badges on her jackets.

Listening

1 Listen and match. What do they collect? 🔊 31

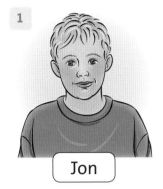 1 Jon

 2 Lisa

 3 Tom and Emma

 4 Jenny

1 ___c___
2 _____
3 _____
4 _____

a 20

b 50

c 100

d 80

Speaking

2 Look at the pictures. Ask and answer.

Has Jon got a collection?

Yes, he has. He's got a shell collection.

How many shells has he got?

He's got one hundred shells.

Writing

Look at the punctuation marks.

Have you got lots of comics**?**

We've got a DVD player**,** a camera and a computer**.**

3 Write the punctuation marks. [.] [,] [?]

1 I collect badges and stickers _._
2 Have you got a sister ___
3 We've got a CD player ___ a computer and a television ___
4 Can I use your camera ___

1 Complete the crossword.

Down

Across

2 Write the correct words.

| fishing | camera | playing |
| season | taking | ~~country~~ |

Anne is nine. She's from Australia. Australia is a hot
¹ _country_ . Anne likes living in Australia. Her favourite
² _____ is summer. Anne likes ³ _____ volleyball
on the beach. She doesn't like ⁴ _____ . She likes
⁵ _____ photos. She's got a great ⁶ _____ .

3 Read and write T (true) or F (false).

1 Akila is from Spain.   _F_
2 Tom and Jack are from the UK. ____
3 Billy is from the USA.   ____
4 Rosa is from Russia.   ____
5 Kate and Ellie are from Australia. ____
6 Olga is from Egypt.   ____

4 Write.

| like | likes | don't like | doesn't like |

Carl	Jo and Sue	Jenny	Lee	Jon and Gary	Emma

1 Carl __likes__ playing volleyball. He __doesn't like__ fishing.

2 Jo and Sue _____ doing gymnastics. They _____ playing the piano.

3 Jenny _____ reading comics. She _____ playing chess.

4 Lee _____ skateboarding. He _____ painting.

5 Jon and Gary _____ taking photos. They _____ playing the guitar.

6 Emma _____ cooking. She _____ shopping.

5 Read and write the numbers.

1 Can I use your MP3 player?

2 Can we have a cake?

3 Can we watch our DVD?

4 Can I play in their garden?

6 Read and complete the words.

| a_e | i_e | o_e | u_e |

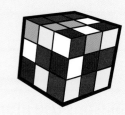
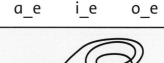

1 I can ride a b_i_k_e_.

2 I've got a puzzle. It's a c__b__.

3 My skipping r__p__ is very long.

4 Look! This doll is from sp__c__.

5 The dog is sitting on a big st__n__.

1 Look at the text. Where are the people? What are they doing?

The Swiss Family Robinson is a novel by Johann David Wyss. It's a very exciting story. The main characters are a mother and father and their four sons, Fritz, Ernest, Jack and Franz. The family decides to travel to a new country to live. They travel on a ship with lots of other people, but there is a big storm. The ship sinks, but the family swim to an island. There aren't any other people on the island, so the family is alone.

They take things from the ship, such as clothes and tools, to help them start a new life. The family has lots of adventures on the island and they learn a lot of important lessons. They find out that the island has everything they need to survive. First, they use wood from the trees to build a house in a tree. When the weather is cold and wet, they move to a cave and make a home there.

They grow vegetables and fruit from seeds and they hunt animals for their meat. They use salt to keep their meat fresh for a long time, so they are never hungry. They cook food on a fire and they use plants to make paper and clothes. They learn a lot about nature and they enjoy their life on the island. One day, they have the chance to leave the island and go home to Switzerland, but they decide that the island is their home now. They are happy with their new life and they don't want to leave.

2 Read and write T (true) or F (false).

1 There are three children in the Robinson family. ____

2 The Robinsons use plants to keep their meat fresh. ____

3 The Robinsons take tools from the ship. ____

4 The Robinsons build a house in a tree. __

3 Look at the texts. Where do you think the children are from? What do you think they do every day?

Families around the world

My name is Riko and I'm from Japan. I live with my parents, my two brothers and our grandparents. We all get up early every morning. After breakfast, my brothers feed our chickens and collect the eggs. Dad and Grandpa pick rice and vegetables in the garden and I help Mum and Grandma to water the flowers and plants. My brothers and I walk to school. We have lessons in the morning and then it's time for lunch. After lunch, we brush our teeth and then we go back to class. In the evening, my family cooks dinner together. All our food comes from our garden. We play games or watch TV after dinner. At bedtime, Mum helps us to get our mattresses out. We keep them in a cupboard during the day so that we have space to play in our rooms.

I'm Ivan and I'm from Russia. I live with my mum, my dad, my grandma and my sister. Our house is in a small village. Mum and Dad go to work every day, so Grandma looks after the house. Grandma makes my breakfast every morning. I usually have bread and tea with honey. Then I walk to school with my friend. We have lessons all morning, but when we need a break we stop working and do some exercises. Lessons finish at lunchtime, and I go home. I take my shoes off before I go into the house. We always wear slippers indoors. After lunch, I ride my bike and then I do my homework. When Dad comes home, he works in the garden. I usually help him. We grow vegetables and fruit. Dad makes bowls, boxes and furniture with wood. He's very clever. In the evenings, I read or watch TV. I go to bed at nine o'clock. I'm always very tired after my busy day.

4 Read and answer the questions.

1 How many brothers has Riko got?

2 How does Ivan get to school?

3 Is your day different to Riko's day? How?

4 Describe your daily routine.

4 We're having fun at the beach!

1 Listen, point and repeat. 🔊 32

swim

sail

dive

surf

kayak

windsurf

snorkel

waterski

2 Listen and read. 🔊 33

Amy Hello, Mum! We're having fun at the beach!
Amy's Mum That's good. Is Max in the sea?
Amy No, he isn't. He's reading his book.

Amy's Mum Is Holly in the sea?
Amy No, she isn't. She's playing with her ball.

Amy Leo is in the sea.
Amy's Mum Oh, yes. Leo likes snorkelling.
Amy He isn't snorkelling. He's surfing. He's very good.
Max Look! Leo is standing on his hands!
Holly Wow!

Max Oh, no! Leo is falling!
Amy Leo isn't surfing now. He's swimming!

1 Listen to the story again and repeat. Act.

2 Look and say.

Let's learn!

I
I'm swimming. I'm **not** swimming.
He / She / It
He's surf**ing**. He **isn't** snorkel**ling**.
You / We / They
We're sail**ing**. They **aren't** waterski**ing**.

This is great! We're sailing!

You aren't sailing!
I'm sailing.

Sometimes the spelling changes:
sail – sail**ing**   play – play**ing**
swim – swim**ming**   run – run**ning**
dive – div**ing**   ride – rid**ing**

3 Read and match.

1 She's windsurfing.

2 They're snorkelling.

3 He's diving.

4 She's waterskiing.

5 He's kayaking.

6 They're surfing.

 a

 b

 c

 d

 e

 f 1

4 Write.

`'s   isn't   're   aren't`

 1

He _isn't_ sleeping.
He _'s_ eating.

 2

She _____ playing
with a ball.
She _____ reading
a book.

 3

They _____ taking photos.
They _____ drawing
pictures.

 4

We _____ swimming.
We _____ windsurfing.

1 Speaking **Look and say.**

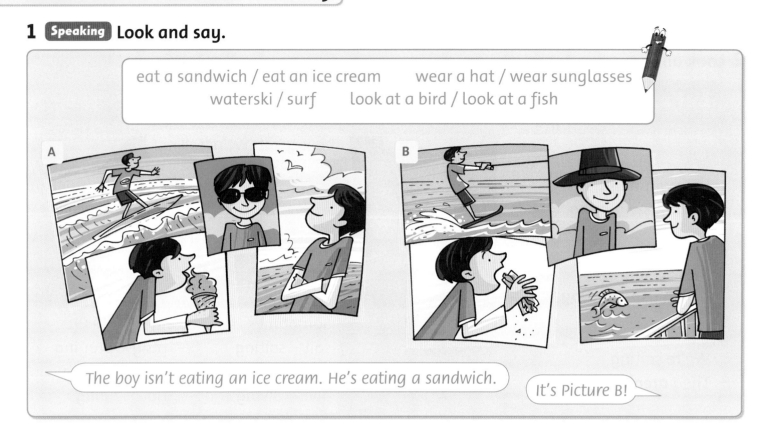

> eat a sandwich / eat an ice cream   wear a hat / wear sunglasses
> waterski / surf   look at a bird / look at a fish

> The boy isn't eating an ice cream. He's eating a sandwich.

> It's Picture B!

2 Write about one of the pictures.

Picture A: The boy is eating an ice cream. He isn't ...

3 Listen and sing. 💿 34

4 Sing and do.

At the beach!

We're playing at the beach today,
We're having lots of fun.
We're swimming and we're surfing,
And we're sitting in the sun.

We all like playing at the beach,
It's sunny here today.
We can windsurf at the beach,
And we can swim and play.

We're sailing in our little boat,
We're playing in the sea.
We're snorkelling and diving,
There are lots of fish to see.

1 Listen, point and repeat. 35

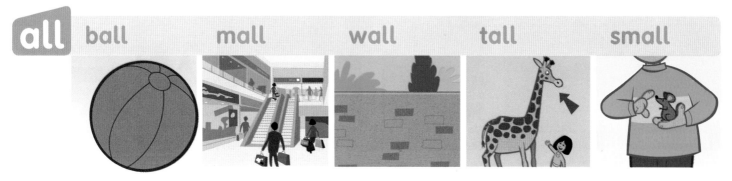

all   ball   mall   wall   tall   small

2 Listen and chant. 36

I'm in a mall,
A mall, mall, mall.
Some people are tall,
Some are small, small, small.
I'm going to buy
A ball, ball, ball.
I don't know which to buy,
I like them all, all, all.

3 Read the chant again. Circle the words with *all*.

4 Match and write.

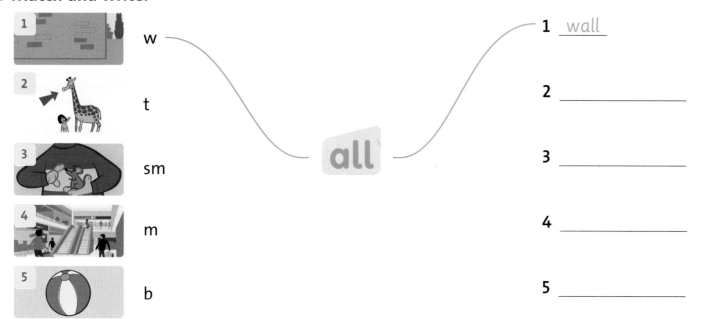

1 w
2 t
3 sm
4 m
5 b

all

1 _wall_
2 _____
3 _____
4 _____
5 _____

Skills Time!

Reading

1 Listen, point and repeat. 🔊 37

polluted

clean

dangerous

safe

beautiful

ugly

2 Look. What can you do with the dolphins?

3 Listen and read. 🔊 38

Dolphin Dreams

Are you looking for the perfect holiday?

Dolphin Dreams is the perfect holiday! We take people in our boats and we visit dolphins in the sea. You can swim with beautiful dolphins!

Do you know ... ?

☼ Dolphins aren't dangerous. They are very friendly. They love playing with people.

☼ Dolphins can't breathe under water, but they can stay under water for about 15 minutes.

☼ Dolphins live in families.

☼ Dolphins have names. Their names are special sounds. They use the sounds to call their friends and family.

☼ Dolphins can't live in polluted water, but a lot of the sea is polluted. We want to make the sea a clean and safe place for dolphins.

BOOK YOUR HOLIDAY TODAY!

4 Read again and write. | dangerous   polluted   clean   ~~beautiful~~ |

1 Dolphins aren't ugly. They are __beautiful__ .

2 Dolphins can't live in polluted water. They live in _____ water.

3 Dolphins are safe. They aren't _____ .

4 A lot of the sea isn't clean. It is _____ .

Listening

1 Listen and write the numbers. 🎧 39

a

b

c

d

e | 1 |

Speaking

2 Ask and answer about you.

| snorkelling   swimming   surfing   diving   waterskiing |
| windsurfing   playing   sailing   kayaking |

What do you like doing at the beach?

I like snorkelling.

Writing

Present continuous verbs – spelling

cook ⟶ cook + ing = cooking

take ⟶ tak~~e~~ + ing = taking

3 Write the correct form of the verbs.

1 I like ___watching___ (watch) dolphins.

2 Do you like _____ (take) photos?

3 I like _____ (cook).

4 Does Joanna like _____ (write) emails?

5 My friend doesn't like _____ (listen) to music.

6 Do you like _____ (read)?

A naughty monkey!

1 Listen, point and repeat. 40

penguin

zebra

monkey

kangaroo

camel

lizard

flamingo

crocodile

2 Listen and read. 41

1

Amy	I love the zoo. I like the penguins.
Holly	Max, I can't see! Are you watching the monkeys?
Max	Yes, I am. They're funny!

2

Holly	Max!
Max	Wait! I'm watching this funny monkey.
Amy	Look! The monkey is taking your sandwich!
Leo	That's my sandwich!

3

Holly	I can't see. Is the monkey eating the sandwich?
Max	No, it isn't. It's taking my book!
Amy	And my bag!

4

Leo	Come here, Holly.
Amy	Look! The monkey is giving our things to Holly.
Max	It likes you!

1 Listen to the story again and repeat. Act.

2 Look and say.

Let's learn!

I

Are you reading?
Yes, I am.   No, I'm not.

He / She / It

Is the monkey eating the sandwich?
Yes, it is.   No, it isn't.

You / We / They

Are they eating?
Yes, they are.   No, they aren't.

Is the crocodile sleeping?

No, it isn't.

3 Read and tick (✔).

1

Is the boy reading?

Yes, he is. ☐

No, he isn't. ✔

2

Are the girls playing chess?

Yes, they are. ☐

No, they aren't. ☐

3

Is the monkey playing with a ball?

Yes, it is. ☐

No, it isn't. ☐

4

Is Mum shopping?

Yes, she is. ☐

No, she isn't. ☐

4 Write.

1 Are the flamingos flying? _No, they aren't._

2 Is the lizard sleeping? _____

3 Is the woman painting? _____

4 Are the monkeys eating bananas? _____

1 **Speaking** **Think of a girl. Ask and answer.**

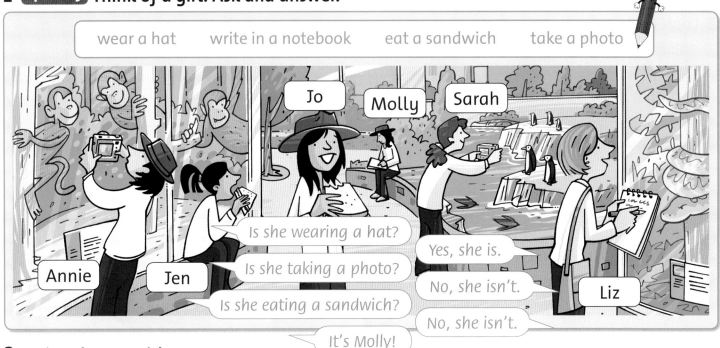

wear a hat   write in a notebook   eat a sandwich   take a photo

Jo   Molly   Sarah

Is she wearing a hat?
Is she taking a photo?
Is she eating a sandwich?

Yes, she is.
No, she isn't.
No, she isn't.

Annie   Jen   Liz

It's Molly!

2 **Write about a girl.**

Annie is taking a photo. She's …

3 **Listen and sing.** 🎧 42

4 **Sing and do.**

Are the monkeys climbing?

Are the monkeys climbing?
Yes, they are.
Are the zebras running?
Yes, they are.
Are the tigers walking?
Are the parrots talking?
Are the monkeys climbing?
Yes, they are.

Are the penguins swimming?
Yes, they are.
Are the parrots flying?
Yes, they are.
Are the lizards eating?
Are the lions sleeping?
Are the penguins swimming?
Yes, they are.

Hello

1 Listen, point and repeat. 🎧 43

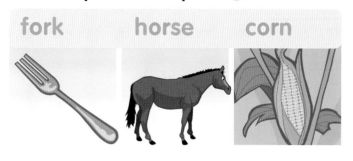

fork	horse	corn

straw	paw	yawn

2 Listen and chant. 🎧 44

Look at the dog.
It's drinking with a straw.
It's holding the straw,
With its two front paws.

Look at the horse,
It's holding a fork.
It's eating corn,
With the farmer's fork.

3 Read the chant again. Circle the words with *or* and *aw*.

4 Circle the odd one out.

1 fork   sport   paw   2 draw   short   straw

3 yawn   horse   corn   4 paw   straw   fork

5 Complete the words with *or* and *aw*.

1	2	3	4	5

str a w   f___k   h___se   p___   y___n

or and aw spellings   Unit 5   **39**

Skills Time!

Reading

1 Listen, point and repeat. 🔊 45

 angry    scared   free   sorry    funny    kind

2 Describe what's happening in the pictures below.

3 Listen and read. 🔊 46

The Lion and the Mouse

1

One day, a lion is sleeping. A mouse runs over the lion's nose and the lion wakes up. The lion is angry. The mouse is scared. "I'm very sorry," says the mouse. "Don't eat me! I can help you one day."

2

The lion laughs. "That's funny!" it says. "You are little! How can you help me?" But the lion is not angry now. The mouse runs away.

3

One year later, the lion is walking in the jungle. A big net falls over the lion. The lion opens its mouth and roars. The mouse hears the lion and it runs to help.

"Don't move," says the mouse. "I can help you."

The mouse chews the net and makes a big hole. The lion is free. "Thank you," says the lion. "You are little, but you are kind."

4 Read again and write.

lion	mouse

1 The _lion_ is sleeping.

2 The _____ is angry.

3 The _____ is little.

4 The _____ opens its mouth and roars.

5 The _____ runs away.

6 The _____ chews a hole in the net.

Listening

1 Listen and write the numbers. 🔊 47

Speaking

2 Look at the pictures. Ask and answer.

| climb | eat | sleep | watch | run |

Is the monkey eating in Picture C?
No, it isn't. It's climbing.

Is the tiger sleeping in Picture C?
No, it isn't. It's eating.

Writing

We use **speech marks** to show that someone is speaking.

"Don't move," says the mouse. "I can help you."

3 Write the speech marks.

1 "Thank you," says the lion.

2 I'm Emma, says the girl.

3 I'm your new teacher, says Mr Brown.

4 These are your desks, he says.
Please sit down.

Lesson One Words

1 Listen, point and repeat. 48

have a shower

brush my teeth

get dressed

have breakfast

brush my hair

get up

catch the bus

walk to school

2 Listen and read. 49

1

Amy I've got an email from Jim! Jim is our cousin in Australia. He's a jackaroo.
Max What's a jackaroo?
Leo Jackaroos work on sheep farms.

2

Amy It's a great job! He gets up early every morning. He rides a horse and he looks after the sheep.

3

Max It's dangerous! There are lots of snakes in Australia. Does Jim see a lot of snakes?
Amy Yes, he does. Look!

4

Leo Jim is lucky. I want to be a jackaroo.
Max I don't! I want a safe job!

1 Listen to the story again and repeat. Act.

2 Look and say.

Let's learn!

I

I **have** breakfast at eight o'clock.
I **don't have** breakfast at seven o'clock.

He / She / It

He **gets** up early.
He **doesn't get** up late.

Does he **live** in a big house?
Yes, he **does.   No**, he **doesn't**.

What time **does** he **start** work?

You / We / They

We **catch** the bus.
They **don't catch** the train.

Do you **walk** to school?
Yes, I **do.   No**, I **don't**.

What time **do** you **go** to school?

Look at Amy. She wants to be a jackaroo!

But jackaroos get up early every morning. Amy doesn't get up early!

3 Read and circle.

1 Billy **get** / **gets up** at seven o'clock.

2 I **has** / **have** breakfast with my family.

3 **Do** / **Does** Katie have a shower in the morning?

4 Fred **doesn't** / **don't** walk to school.

5 My mum and dad **doesn't** / **don't** catch the bus to work.

6 **Do** / **Does** your friends brush their teeth at night?

4 Write.

Jack _gets up_ (get up) at seven o'clock.

Emma _____ (brush) her teeth every morning.

Jen and Jo _____ (not catch) the bus to school.

Tom _____ (have) breakfast with his family.

1 (Speaking) **Ask and answer.**

What time does Tom get up?

He gets up at half past seven.

2 Write about Tom.

Tom gets up at half past seven. He ...

3 Listen and sing. 🔊 50

4 Sing and do.

My day

I get up early every day,
I have a shower every day,
I have my breakfast every day,
I'm busy all day long.

I catch the school bus every day,
I have my lessons every day,
I see my school friends every day,
I'm busy all day long.

I do my homework every day,
Then I go outside and play,
I'm very busy every day,
I'm busy all day long.

1 Listen, point and repeat. 🔊 51

boy   toy   oyster   coin   oil   soil

2 Listen and chant. 🔊 52

Roy is a boy,
A boy, boy, boy.

Playing with a toy,
A toy, toy, toy.

He can see a coin,
A coin, coin, coin.

3 Read the chant again. Circle the words with *oy* and *oi*.

4 Match and write.

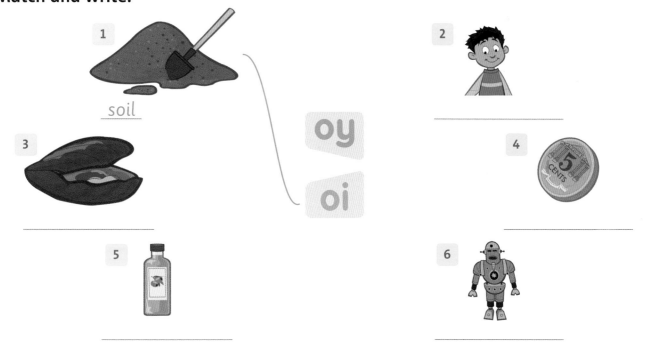

1 soil

2 _____

oy

oi

3 _____

4 _____

5 _____

6 _____

Skills Time!

Reading

1 Listen, point and repeat. 🎧 53

| first | then | next | finally | every day | at the weekend |

2 Look at the text. Where does Ellie live?

3 Listen and read. 🎧 54

Cyber School

Australia is a very big country. A lot of families live on farms. The farms are a long way from towns or cities, so the children don't go to school. They have lessons at home and they talk to their teachers on the Internet. They are students of the Cyber School!

Ellie, 10

I live on a farm. There isn't a town for 500 kilometres! That's six hours in the car! So I do Cyber School. I get up early every day. First, I help on the farm. Then, I watch my teachers on the Internet. Next, I do my school work. Finally, I email my work to my teacher. Some of my school friends live 2,000 kilometres away! But we meet every year and have a sports day together!

4 Read again and answer the questions.

1 Does Ellie live in a town? _No._

2 Does Ellie email her work? _____

3 Does Ellie get up late? _____

4 Does Ellie live close to her friends? _____

5 Does Ellie watch her teachers on the Internet? _____

6 Does Ellie see her friends at the weekend? _____

Listening

1 Listen and write the numbers. 🔊 55

Speaking

2 Ask and answer about you.

get up   have breakfast   start school
finish school   have dinner   go to bed

What time do you get up?

I get up at half past seven.

What time do you have breakfast?

I have breakfast at quarter to eight.

Writing

Proper nouns are names of people or places, and titles of books or films. Proper nouns start with capital letters.

Noun	Proper noun
girl	Ellie
teacher	Mr Green
country	Egypt
city	London
book	Family and Friends
film	Toy Story

3 Read and circle the proper nouns.

1 Ellie lives in Australia.
2 Mrs Smith is my new teacher.
3 Carlos is from Spain.
4 My favourite film is The Incredibles.
5 Cairo is the capital city of Egypt.
6 Helen's favourite film is Finding Nemo.
7 Jen is older than Beth.

1 Complete the crossword.

Down

1
2
4
7

Across

3
5
6
8

Crossword answers shown:
1 Down: m o n k e y
5 Across: n
6 Across
3 Across
8 Across: n
7 Down: f

2 Write the correct words.

| zebra | kangaroo | camel | crocodile | flamingo | ~~lizard~~ |

Look at the animals! The ¹ _lizard_ is sleeping in the sun. The ² _____ is swimming in the water. The ³ _____ is flying. The ⁴ _____ is jumping. Can you see it? The ⁵ _____ is running It's very fast. The ⁶ _____ is hungry. It's eating.

3 Read and circle.

1 Dad **is** / (**isn't**) reading a book.

2 The girls **are** / **aren't** listening to music.

3 The boys **are** / **aren't** playing chess.

4 Mum **is** / **isn't** watching TV.

5 Dad **is** / **isn't** eating an apple.

6 The boys **are** / **aren't** listening to music.

4 Match the questions with the answers.

1 Is Tom watching a DVD? [d]
2 Are the children playing volleyball? [ ]
3 Is Katie snorkelling? [ ]
4 Are you and your friends surfing? [ ]
5 Is the monkey jumping? [ ]
6 Are you eating a sandwich, Lee? [ ]

a Yes, she is.
b No, it isn't.
c Yes, I am.
d No, he isn't.
e Yes, we are.
f No, they aren't.

1 _d_   2 ___   3 ___   4 ___   5 ___   6 ___

5 Complete the text. | gets   brushes   plays   walks   catches   ~~has~~ |

Billy gets up at seven o'clock on Mondays. He ¹ _has_ a
shower and then he ² _____ dressed. He has breakfast with
his family. He always ³ _____ his teeth after breakfast.
He never ⁴ _____ the bus to school. He always ⁵ _____ to
school with his brother. After school, he ⁶ _____ with his
friends in the park. Billy loves the park!

6 Read and complete the words. | aw   or   oy   oi |

A cat hasn't got hands or
feet, it's got four p _a_ _w_ s.

Flowers and trees grow
in s ___ ___ l.

The farmer has got
a big f ___ ___ k.

"What a big y ___ ___ n!"
"Yes, I'm very tired."

My favourite t ___ ___ is my
new train.

There is ___ ___ l in this
bottle.

Extensive reading: Animals

1 Look at the picture. What is the wolf doing?

The wolf pups are hungry, but their mother can't find enough food. Soon, there is only one pup left. He drinks his mother's milk and slowly grows stronger. He is fierce, but he is playful, too. When his mother leaves the cave to look for food, he explores the cave, but he is afraid to go outside. However, as he grows older, he wants to find out what the world is like outside the cave. He learns to hide in the long grass or in the bushes. He learns to hunt and he catches small animals to eat. Other animals try to attack him, but he learns to fight. His mother is proud of him. She can see that he is becoming a great wolf.

One day, while the young wolf is exploring, he comes to a village. He sees a group of men and he is afraid. One of the men tries to pick him up. The pup growls and shows his sharp, white teeth. The men laugh.
"Look at those teeth," they say. "Let's call him White Fang."

Another man tries to pick White Fang up, but White Fang bites the man's hand. The man hits White Fang and White Fang cries. His mother hears him and comes to find him. When she sees the men, she lies down on the ground. She respects humans. A man decides to keep White Fang and his mother. At first, White Fang wants to escape. But the man feeds White Fang and gives him a dry place to sleep. When other dogs try to attack White Fang, the man chases them away.

"Men can protect me and care for me," White Fang thinks. "It is difficult to be a wolf, but it is easy to be a dog."

2 Read and match the sentence halves.

1 The young wolf explores the cave ☐
2 The men call the wolf White Fang ☐
3 White Fang thinks it's easy to be a dog ☐
4 White Fang's mother lies in the ground ☐

a because men can protect him.
b because he has sharp white teeth.
c when his mother leaves to find food.
d because she respects humans.

3 Look at the picture. Where is the polar bear?

Flocke
the polar bear

Nuremberg Zoo is a huge zoo in Germany. There are about 300 species of animals there. The zoo has got lots of special enclosures for gorillas, leopards and polar bears. The enclosures have got rocks, trees and pools for the animals. More than one million visitors come to the zoo every year, and they all want to meet Flocke.

Flocke is a polar bear. She is two years old. Her name is German and it means 'snowflake'. The keepers at Nuremberg zoo take baby polar bears away from their mothers and look after them because mother polar bears sometimes hurt their babies. Flocke spends a lot of time with her keepers, so she is very friendly. She has got a lot of fans because she is so beautiful and gentle.

Flocke is not a baby now, so her keepers want her to spend more time on her own. They want her to live with other bears instead of humans. Flocke is very happy in the polar bear enclosure at Nuremberg Zoo. She enjoys playing and swimming in her pool. She also loves eating sweet fruits. She likes grapes, melons, and pears, but bananas are her favourites.

The zoo has got a website about Flocke. They put news and photos on the website so that Flocke's fans can learn more about her. People can buy games, diaries, postcards with Flocke's picture on them. There are also DVDs about Flocke and soft toy polar bears. The money from all these Flocke items helps to protect animals around the world.

4 Read and write T (true) or F (false).

1 Flocke is friendly. ___   2 Flocke is four years old. ___

3 Flocke doesn't like bananas. ___   4 Flocke has got a pool. ___

Lesson One Words

1 Listen, point and repeat. 🔊 56

café

library

museum

playground

shopping mall

sports centre

swimming pool

cinema

2 Listen and read. 🔊 57

1

Mum	What do you want to do at the weekend?
Holly	Can we go to the shopping mall?
Leo	Oh, no!

2

Amy	Can we go to the sports centre?
Max	But we always go to the sports centre!

3

Max	Can we go to the museum?
Holly	I don't like museums!
Leo	We never want to do the same thing!

4

Dad	Surprise! I've got tickets for the new film at the cinema at the weekend!
Amy & Leo	Great!
Max & Holly	Wow, thanks, Dad!
Mum	So, now you want to do the same thing!

1 Listen to the story again and repeat. Act.

2 Look and say.

Let's learn!

We **always** go to the sports centre.
I **sometimes** go to the library.
She **never** goes to the shopping mall.

My birthday is **in** May.
He plays football **on** Fridays.
We get up **at** eight o'clock.

We always go to the playground on Saturdays.

3 Read and circle.   ✔✔ = always   ✔ = sometimes   ✗ = never

Billy **never** / **always** rides his bike to school.

They **never** / **sometimes** watch TV.

Tom **sometimes** / **always** takes photos.

Mum **sometimes** / **never** listens to music.

4 Write.   on   in   at

1 Emma's birthday is _in_ March.

2 I always have lunch _____ one o'clock.

3 Dad never works _____ Saturdays.

4 We sometimes go to the beach _____ August.

5 You never watch TV _____ Mondays.

6 The children always go to bed _____ nine o'clock.

1 Speaking **Think of a boy or a girl. Look and say.**

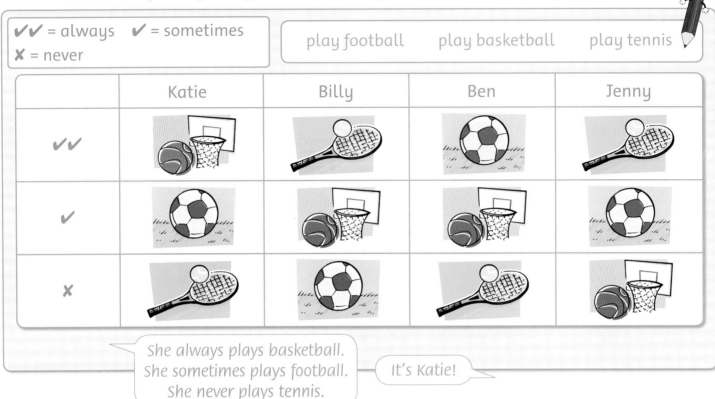

| ✔✔ = always ✔ = sometimes ✘ = never | play football   play basketball   play tennis |

She always plays basketball.
She sometimes plays football.
She never plays tennis.

It's Katie!

2 **Write about Billy, Ben or Jenny.**

Katie sometimes plays football. She never plays tennis. She ...

3 **Listen and sing.** 58

4 **Sing and do.**

Come and play with me!

I sometimes play computer games,
I always ride my bike.
I sometimes watch a DVD,
I sometimes fly my kite.

I sometimes snorkel in the sea,
I sometimes read a book.
I always play my new guitar,
I never shop or cook.

I sometimes surf the Internet,
I sometimes watch TV.
I always have a lot of fun,
So come and play with me!

1 Listen, point and repeat. 🎧 59

cow   clown   flower   house   trousers   mouse

2 Listen and chant. 🎧 60

The (clown's) got flowers,
Red and blue.
He's wearing brown trousers,
But only one shoe.

He's sitting in his house,
He looks behind a wall.
He's scared of a mouse,
But it's only small.

3 Read the chant again. Circle the words with *ow* and *ou*.

4 Circle the odd one out.

1 cow   (house)   flower   2 clown   cow   trousers
3 flower   house   mouse   4 house   clown   trousers

5 Write the words in the correct box.

~~brown~~   out   down   clown   shout   cloud   trousers   flower

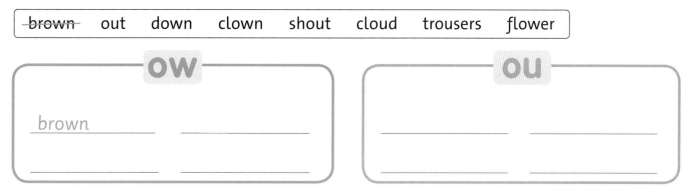

ow

brown _____   _____

_____   _____

ou

_____   _____

_____   _____

Reading

1 Listen, point and repeat. 🔊 61

play

theatre

concert

actor

film

singer

2 Look at the text. Where can you see the film?

3 Listen and read. 🔊 62

DREAM CASTLE

Dream Castle is a wonderful new film at the Sunshine Cinema!

In the film, Katie and her brother Harry visit their uncle. Their uncle lives in a big, old castle. One day, Katie and Harry find a very big, old door. They open the door and go into the room.

In the room, a princess is sleeping in a big bed. The princess thinks she is living one hundred years ago!

Katie and Harry try to hide the princess from their uncle. It is very difficult and they all have lots of funny adventures!

Dream Castle is a film but the actors also sing! Here is what some people think:

The film has got a good story and it's very exciting!
Jack, 9

The actors in the film are very good. They are great singers too!
Emma, 8

4 Read again and answer the questions.

1 Do Katie and Harry visit their grandpa? _No._

2 Do the actors sing in the film? _____

3 Do Katie and Harry find a princess? _____

4 Do Katie and Harry try and hide the princess? _____

5 Is the princess sleeping in a small bed? _____

6 Is the film sad? _____

Listening

1 Listen and tick (✔) or cross (✘). 🎧 63

Speaking

2 Ask and answer about you.

> watching films / go to the cinema   listening to music / go to concerts
> playing sports / go to the sports centre   reading / go to the library
> shopping / go to the shopping mall

Do you like watching films?   *Yes, I do.*

Do you ever go to the cinema?   *Yes, I sometimes go to the cinema.*

Writing

Verbs show actions:

walk   read   cook

Adjectives describe nouns.

big cake   old house   nice day

Prepositions describe place, time and movement.

on the table   at ten o'clock
to school

3 Circle the verbs in red, the adjectives in blue and the prepositions in green.

1 Their aunt and uncle live in a very big castle.

2 Jack is riding his new bike to school today.

3 I live in a small flat.

4 I swim in the sea on sunny days.

5 School starts at 9 o'clock.

6 The cake on the table is great.

Lesson One Words

1 Listen, point and repeat. 🔊 64

pasta

bread

cereal

meat

melon

cucumber

onion

lemon

2 Listen and read. 🔊 65

1

Amy	Wow! This is a big supermarket!
Max	I like shopping at the supermarket. Mum and I come here every week.
Mum	We need a lot of things today. Can you help me, please?
Amy	Sure.

2

Mum	We need some pasta and some bread.
Amy	The bread is over there.
Mum	Can you get me some onions and a cucumber, please?
Max	OK.

3

Amy	Oh, there are melons, too. I'd like a melon.

4

Max	No, Amy! Don't take that melon! Take one from the top!
Amy	Oh, no! Sorry!

1 Listen to the story again and repeat. Act.

2 Look and say.

Let's learn!

countable noun	uncountable noun
one melon	some bread
two melons three melons some melons	

I / You / He / She / It / We / They

I'd like a melon.
We'd like some pasta.

Would you like some cereal?
Yes, please.   No, thanks.

I'd like = I **would** like

Would you like a banana?

No, thanks.

We'd like an ice cream!

3 Choose _a_, _an_ or _some_. Write the words in the correct boxes.

apple   salad   bread
biscuit   egg   fries
rice   water   milkshake
pasta   melon   orange

Countable	Uncountable
an apple	some salad

4 Write.   a   an   some

Edward would like _a_ sandwich.

The children would like _____ pastries.

'Would your friends like _____ drinks?'

She would like _____ apple.

Lesson Three Grammar and Song

1 **Speaking** **Think of a boy or a girl. Look and say.**

pasta   bread   cereal   meat
melon   cucumber   onion   lemon

Stacy   Ollie   Emma   Tom   Isobel   Harry

He'd like some meat, a melon
and a cucumber.

It's Ollie!

2 **Write about two people.**

Ollie would like some meat, a melon and a cucumber.

3 **Listen and sing.** 🔊 66

4 **Sing and do.**

At the supermarket

I would like some lemons,
I would like some meat.
I would like a melon,
They're very fresh and sweet.

At the supermarket
We buy things to eat.
Apples, bread and biscuits,
Pasta, rice and meat.

I would like some onions,
I would like some rice.
I would like some apples,
They're healthy and they're nice.

1 Listen, point and repeat. 67

ld child shield field

lt belt quilt adult

2 Listen and chant. 68

A child and an adult
Are standing in a field.
The adult's got a quilt.
The child's got a shield.

The quilt is red,
The shield is grey.
The adult sits down,
But the child wants to play.

3 Read the chant again. Circle the words with *ld* and *lt*.

4 Match and write.

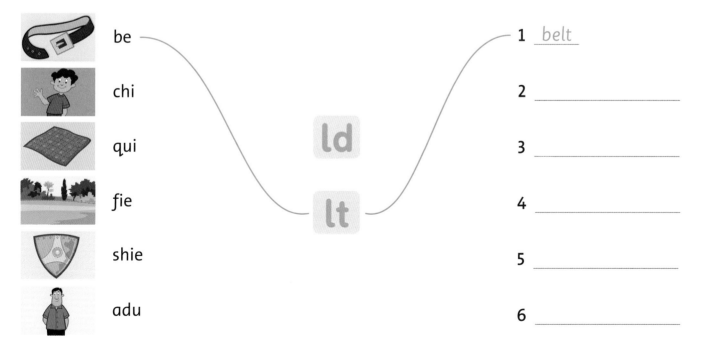

be
chi
qui
fie
shie
adu

ld
lt

1 belt
2 _____
3 _____
4 _____
5 _____
6 _____

Reading

1 Listen, point and repeat. 🎧 69

 potato
 butter
 cheese
 salt
 pepper
 peas

2 What food can you see in the pictures below?

3 Listen and read. 🎧 70

My Favourite Dish

Today I want to tell you,
How to make my favourite dish.
You need two big potatoes,
And you need a piece of fish.

You need some milk and butter,
And you need a lot of cheese.
You need some salt and pepper,
And you need some nice fresh peas.

You cook the two potatoes,
And you mash them in a pot.
You cook the peas in water,
And you make them nice and hot.

You cook the fish in milk now,
And you put it in a dish.
You take the peas and butter,
And you mix them with the fish.

You add the mashed potatoes,
And you put the cheese on top.
You cook it in the oven,
When it's brown on top, you stop!

4 Read again and write *T* (true) or *F* (false).

1 You need two small potatoes. _F_
2 You need a piece of meat. ____
3 You need some butter. ____
4 You cook the peas in milk. ____
5 You put the fish in a dish. ____
6 You put the cheese on top. ____

Listening

1 Listen and write *A* or *B*. 🔊 71

1 _B_   2 _____   3 _____   4 _____   5 _____   6 _____

Speaking

2 Look at the pictures. Ask and answer.

What would you like?

I'd like some potatoes, please. And I'd like …

Writing

> **We put adjectives describing size before** adjectives describing colour.
> I can see a   big,   white   bird.

3 Put the words in the correct columns. Then write the sentences.

~~big~~   ~~green~~   small   red   pink   little   tall   blue

Size	Colour
big	green

1 You need two _big, red_ tomatoes. (red / big)
2 Mum is wearing a _____ hat. (little / pink)
3 Look at the _____ trees. (green / tall)
4 We're sailing in a _____ boat. (small / blue)

Lesson One Words

1 Listen, point and repeat. 72

lake

mountain

waterfall

ocean

wide

big

deep

high

2 Listen and read. 73

1

Teacher	Hello. I've got a quiz for you today!
Max	Great!

2

Teacher	What's the highest mountain in the world?
Max	Mount Everest.
Teacher	That's right! What's the biggest ocean in the world?
Max	It's the Pacific Ocean!
Teacher	That's right!

3

Teacher	What's the fastest animal in the world?
Amy	A mouse!
Teacher	No! A mouse isn't the fastest animal. The fastest animal in the world is a cheetah.

4

Amy	No! A mouse! Look!
Max	Ha ha! Now Amy is the fastest student in the class!

1 **Listen to the story again and repeat. Act.**

2 **Look and say.**

Let's learn!

The Nile is long**er than** the Volga.
The Pacific Ocean is wid**er than** the Atlantic Ocean.
Russia is big**ger than** the UK.

What's the fast**est** animal in the world?

The fast**est** animal in the world is the cheetah.
The Pacific Ocean is **the** wid**est** ocean in the world.
Russia is **the** big**gest** country in the world.

> My sandcastle is bigger than your sandcastle, Max!

> Look, Amy! My sandcastle is the biggest!

3 **Read and write *T* (true) or *F* (false).**

1 Tom is the tallest boy. _T_
2 Colin is faster than Tom. ___
3 Billy is the fastest boy. ___
4 Tom is slower than Colin. ___
5 Billy is taller than Colin. ___
6 Colin is the shortest boy. ___

Colin   Tom   Billy

4 **Write.**

1 The USA is _bigger_ (big) than Spain.
2 Mount Everest is the _____ (high) mountain in the world.
3 Cars are _____ (fast) than bikes.
4 Grapes are _____ (small) than apples.
5 Lake Baikal is the _____ (deep) lake in the world.
6 Mice are _____ (slow) than cheetahs.

1 `Speaking` **Ask and answer.**

Biggest fruit	Fastest transport	Tallest animal	Smallest country	Slowest animal
a grape	a car	a cat	the UK	a monkey
an apple	a plane	a giraffe	the USA	a cheetah
a melon	a train	a lion	Russia	a horse

What's the slowest animal?

A monkey!

2 Write three sentences.

The slowest animal is a monkey. The ...

3 Listen and sing. 74

4 Sing and do.

My quiz

What's the biggest country?
Do you know? Do you know?
What's the highest mountain?
Do you know?
Listen to my quiz,
Listen to my quiz and
Tell me what the answer is!

Do you know? Do you know?
Do you know what the answer is?
Listen to my quiz,
Listen to my quiz and
Tell me what the answer is!

What's the biggest ocean?
Do you know? Do you know?
What's the smallest country?
Do you know?
Listen to my quiz,
Listen to my quiz and
Tell me what the answer is!

1 **Listen, point and repeat.** 🔊 75

2 **Listen and chant.** 🔊 76

. We put up the tent
At the big, big camp.
We hear the wind.
We light the lamp.

We sit by the pond.
We look at the plants.
We're happy together,
Just me and my aunt.

3 **Read the chant again. Circle the words with *nd*, *nt* and *mp*.**

4 **Circle the end letters *nd*, *nt* or *mp* below.**

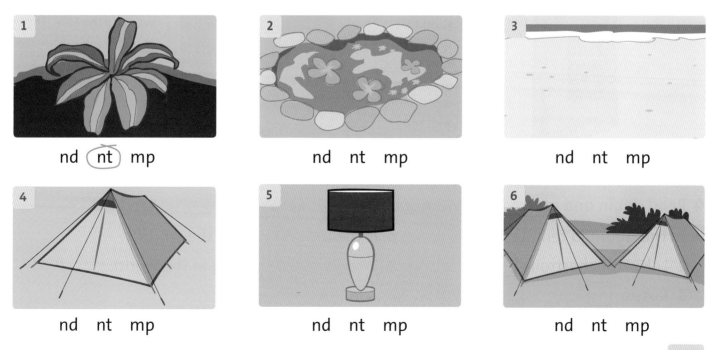

nd (nt) mp   nd   nt   mp   nd   nt   mp

nd   nt   mp   nd   nt   mp   nd   nt   mp

Skills Time!

Reading

1 Listen, point and repeat. 🔊 77

building

country

bridge

river

old

long

2 Describe what you can see in the pictures below.

3 Listen and read. 🔊 78

World Records

**Here are some of the world's records!
There are many interesting facts!**

The Ggantija temples are in Malta. The temples are over 5,500 years old! They are the oldest buildings in the world!

The longest bridges in the world are the two bridges over Lake Pontchartrain in the USA. The bridges are nearly 24 miles long. You can't see land from the middle of the bridges!

Russia is the biggest country in the world. It is 17,075,400 square kilometres! That is 12.5% of the earth's surface! In Russia, there are eleven different time zones. Russia is between Europe and Asia.

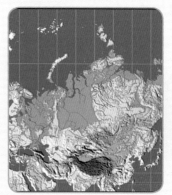

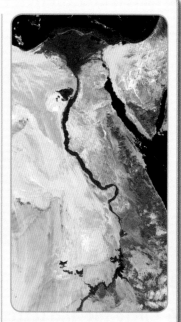

The longest river in the world is the Nile. The Nile is 6,695 kilometres long. The Nile flows through nine countries in Africa. The last country is Egypt. From Egypt, it flows into the Mediterranean Sea.

4 Read again and match the sentence halves.

1 The Ggantija temples [d]
2 Lake Pontchartrain [ ]
3 Russia [ ]
4 The Nile [ ]

a is the longest river in the world.
b is the biggest country in the world.
c is in the USA.
d are the oldest buildings in the world.

Listening

1 Listen and complete the table. 🎧 79

| Egypt | Brazil | the UK | Spain |

Country	_____	_Egypt_	_____	_____
Biggest lake	Lake Sanabria	Lake Nasser	Loch Neagh	Lake Patos
Longest river	The Tagus	The Nile	The Severn	The Amazon
Highest mountain	Mount Teide	Mount Catherine	Ben Nevis	Fog Peak

Speaking

2 Ask and answer. | long   big   high |

What's the biggest lake in Spain?

Lake Sanabria.

What's the longest river in Spain?

The Tagus.

What's the highest mountain in Spain?

Mount Teide.

Writing

Adverbs of frequency tell us how often something happens.
We usually put adverbs of frequency before the verb.

I always go to the shopping mall.
I never go to the shopping mall.

Some adverbs of frequency can go at the beginning or the end of a sentence.

I sometimes go to the shopping mall.
I go to the shopping mall sometimes.
Sometimes I go to the shopping mall.

3 Are these sentences correct?
Read and tick (✔) or cross (✗).

1 I always go to Lake Sanabria on holiday. ✔
2 Alison cooks never. ☐
3 You watch DVDs sometimes. ☐
4 The boys play football always. ☐
5 Always I go swimming on Saturdays. ☐
6 She sometimes plays chess. ☐
7 They never eat Italian food. ☐

Review 3

1 Complete the crossword.

Down

Across

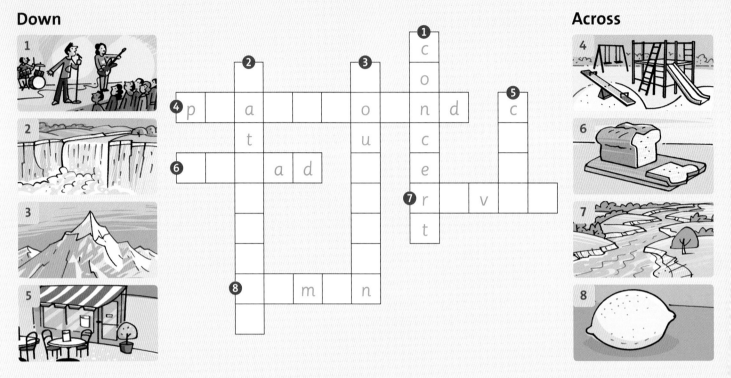

2 Write the correct words.

| café | library | shopping mall | sports centre | cinema | ~~swimming pool~~ |

Lisa does lots of things at the weekend. She always goes swimming at the [1] _swimming pool_. She sometimes shops at the [2] _____ and she sometimes watches a film at the [3] _____. She always eats ice cream at the [4] _____ with her friends and she sometimes reads books at the [5] _____. She always plays tennis at the [6] _____, too. Lisa loves weekends!

3 Complete the sentences.

✔✔ = always   ✔ = sometimes   ✗ = never

1 Katie _sometimes_ (✔) reads comics.

2 The boys _____ (✗) go to the museum.

3 You _____ (✔✔) ride your bike to school.

4 Jack _____ (✔) plays football in the park.

5 We _____ (✔✔) have breakfast in the morning.

6 My friends _____ (✗) watch films.

4 Write.

a	an	some

There is lots of food on the table. There is
¹ _some_ pasta and there is ² _____ onion.
There are ³ _____ lemons and there is
⁴ _____ cucumber. There is ⁵ _____
bread and there is ⁶ _____ melon, too.

5 Complete the sentences.

1 The monkey is _bigger_ (big) than the mouse.
2 The mouse is the _____ (small) animal.
3 The cheetah is the _____ (big) animal.
4 The mouse is _____ (fast) than the monkey.
5 The cheetah is the _____ (fast) animal.

6 Read and complete the words.

ld	lt	nd	nt	mp

In my garden there are
flowers, trees and pla _n_ _t_ s.

On my trousers I wear a
be __ __ .

There is a la __ __ on the
table next to my bed.

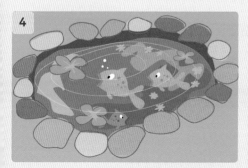

There are lots of fish in the
po __ __ .

I've got a red qui __ __ on
my bed.

The family is having a
picnic in the fie __ __ .

1 Look at the picture. What are the people doing?

Some travellers arrived in a small village one day. They were tired and hungry, but they didn't have any food. They only had a large pot. The travellers asked the villagers for some food, but the villagers didn't trust the travellers and they didn't want to share their food.

The travellers were disappointed, but they had a plan. They filled their pot with water, dropped a large stone into it and put the pot on a fire in the village square. Then the travellers sat down around the fire and waited. Soon, a woman came to the square.

"What are you doing?" she asked. "We're making stone soup," said the travellers. "It's very tasty, but we really need some herbs to put in it."

"I've got some herbs," said the woman. "Can you give us some of your herbs?" the travellers asked. "Then we will share our soup with you."

The woman took a small bunch of fresh herbs from her basket and dropped it into the pot. She sat with the travellers and they talked while they waited for the soup to cook. After a while, a man came to the square. "What are you doing?" he asked. "We're making stone soup," said the travellers. "It's delicious, but we really need some meat to put in it."

"I've got some meat," said the man. "Can you give us some of your meat?" the travellers asked. "Then we will share our soup with you." The man put some meat into the pot, then he sat with the travellers and the woman and they all talked while they waited for the soup to cook.

More villagers came to the square. They all added food to the pot. Soon, they were good friends. The pot was full of meat, potatoes and vegetables, and it smelt wonderful. The travellers and the villagers shared the soup and they all enjoyed a wonderful meal.

2 Read and answer the questions.

1 What did the travellers ask?   2 Why were the travellers disappointed?

3 What did the man put in the pot?   4 What did the woman put in the pot?

3 Look at the pictures. Where do you think these dishes are from?

National dishes

Sarma

Sarma is a national dish of Bulgaria, but people make similar dishes in many other countries, such as Egypt, Greece, Turkey, Romania and Russia. The dish has different names in different countries. People in Egypt call it *mahshi* and people in Greece call it *dolmades*. To make the dish, people mix minced meat, rice, onions, salt, pepper and herbs together. They wrap the mixture in large cabbage leaves to make little parcels. Then, they put the parcels in a large pot and boil them for several hours. When the parcels are ready, people serve them with rice or potatoes. They often add yoghurt, too. Sometimes people use leaves from different plants to wrap the meat and rice. One popular recipe uses vine leaves. People in different countries like to add different things to the recipe. Sometimes people use vegetables instead of meat, or serve the parcels in a tasty tomato sauce. The dish is often different, but always delicious.

Ceviche

Ceviche is one of Peru's national dishes. It is raw fish (or cooked shellfish) in citrus juice. Citrus fruits include lemons, limes, grapefruits and oranges. People usually use lemons or limes to make *ceviche*. They put pieces of fish in the lime or lemon juice with sliced onion, garlic and hot peppers. You can use lots of different kinds of fish. One traditional recipe for *ceviche* uses shark meat. The citrus juice 'cooks' the fish without heat. When the fish is in the citrus juice, you can see it turn from pink to white. When the fish is white, the dish is ready. *Ceviche* is very quick and easy to make. It is ready in just a few minutes. People in Peru usually serve *ceviche* with corn, potato or seaweed. It is also popular in other countries in Latin America, such as Ecuador, Chile, Mexico and Cuba.

4 Read and answer the questions.

1 Where do people eat *sarma / mahshi*?
2 What are the ingredients in *ceviche*?
3 Have you ever cooked a dish? What?
4 What's your favourite dish? What are the ingredients?

10 In the park!

1 Listen, point and repeat. 🔊 80

path

grass

flowers

bin

trees

playground

fountain

litter

2 Listen and read. 🔊 81

1

Amy   This is a beautiful park.
Max   Yes, it is. I love it here.
Holly   Oh, look at the flowers!
Leo   Holly, you mustn't pick the flowers.
Holly   Oh, OK.

2

Holly   Oh, look at the little trees!
Max   You mustn't walk on the grass here, Holly. You must walk on the path.
Holly   Oh, OK.

3

Amy   Holly! Let's play with this ball.
Max   No, you mustn't play here.
Amy   Well, let's go to the playground. We can play there. Catch the ball, Max!

4

Holly   Oh, Max! You mustn't play in the fountain!
Max   Ha ha. Very funny.

1 Listen to the story again and repeat. Act.

2 Look and say.

Let's learn!

I / You / He / She / It / We / They

We **must** do our homework.
They **mustn't** talk in class.

You **must** turn off your mobile phone.
You **mustn't** walk on the grass.

mustn't = must **not**

Sometimes 'you' means everyone.

Max! You must look in front of you!

Yes, Max. You mustn't walk and read your book.

3 Read and match.

1 You mustn't walk your dog here.   2 You must put litter in the bin.

3 You mustn't take photos here.   4 You must be quiet.

a

b

c

d 1

4 Write. | must   mustn't |

1 You _mustn't_ eat here.   2 You _____ wash your hands.

3 You _____ turn off your mobile   4 You _____ swim here.
   phone here.

1

2

3

4

1 **Speaking** Look and say.

turn off your mobile phone   put litter in the bin   walk on the grass
be quiet   walk your dog   wash your hands   take photos   eat here

You must put litter in the bin.
It's Picture 1!
You mustn't walk on the grass.
It's Picture 3!

2 Write four sentences.

You must put litter in the bin. You …

3 Listen and sing. 🔘 82

4 Sing and do.

You must come to the park

Oh, you must come to the park,
So we can have some fun.
You must come to the park today,
And play games in the sun.

Oh, we must walk on the path,
And we mustn't climb the trees.
We must put litter in the bin,
Let's keep the park clean, please.

Oh, we must be very good,
And we mustn't pick the flowers.
But we can have a lot of fun,
And play for hours and hours.

1 Listen, point and repeat. 🔊 83

rain   train   Monday   tray   case   race

2 Listen and chant. 🔊 84

It's Monday today,
And I can play.

Outside there's rain,
But I'm in with my trains.

I open my case,
And the trains have a race!

3 Read the chant again. Circle the words with *ai*, *ay* and *a_e*.

4 Match and write.

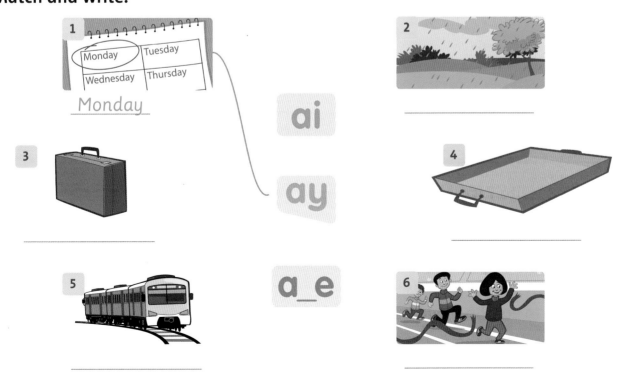

1 Monday | Tuesday
   Wednesday | Thursday
   Monday

ai

ay

a_e

Reading

1 Listen, point and repeat. 🔊 85

| shout | chase | catch | meet | cross | laugh |

2 Describe what's happening in the pictures below.

3 Listen and read. 🔊 86

THE GINGERBREAD MAN

One day, an old woman makes a Gingerbread Man. When it is ready, the old woman wants to eat him. But the Gingerbread Man laughs and shouts "Run, run, run if you can. You can't catch me! I'm the Gingerbread Man!" The old woman is angry. She chases him.

The Gingerbread Man meets a cat. The cat wants to eat him, but he runs away. He runs to the river. He wants to cross the river but he can't swim.

There is a fox near the river. "I can swim," says the fox. "Sit on my head." The Gingerbread Man sits on the fox's head. The fox starts to swim. "The water is deeper now," says the fox. "You must sit on my nose." The Gingerbread Man sits on the fox's nose. And the fox opens its mouth and eats him!

4 Read again and write _T_ (true) or _F_ (false).

1 The old woman makes a Gingerbread Man.   T

2 The old woman runs away.   ___

3 The Gingerbread Man meets a monkey.   ___

4 The cat wants to eat the Gingerbread Man.   ___

5 The Gingerbread Man can swim.   ___

6 The fox eats the Gingerbread Man.   ___

Listening

1 Listen and write the numbers. 87

Speaking

2 Look at the pictures. Play the game.

> eat   be quiet   turn off your mobile phone
> run   put the books on the shelf

You mustn't eat in the library.

It's Picture A!

Writing

We use and / or to link two ideas in a sentence.
We use and in positive sentences and or in negative sentences.

Lisa likes apples and bananas.
Tim doesn't play football or basketball.

3 Write *and* or *or*.

1 The Gingerbread Man doesn't like the woman _or_ the cat.

2 I don't walk _____ ride my bike to school.

3 He reads comics _____ books.

4 I've got an English lesson _____ a maths lesson on Monday.

Lesson One Words

1 Listen, point and repeat. 🔊 88

ferry

bus

helicopter

motorbike

plane

taxi

train

tram

2 Listen and read. 🔊 89

1

Holly What's this? Is it a tram?
Max No, it isn't. It's a horse bus. There were horse buses two hundred years ago.

2

Amy Look at these! There were some funny trains a hundred years ago!
Leo Wow! There were skateboards fifty years ago! And they were very big!

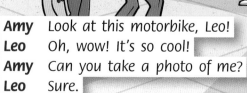

3

Amy Look at this motorbike, Leo!
Leo Oh, wow! It's so cool!
Amy Can you take a photo of me?
Leo Sure.

4

Max Leo! That man is looking at your skateboard.
Man Wow! Look! This skateboard is fifty years old!
Leo No, sorry. That's my skateboard. It's only two years old.

1 Listen to the story again and repeat. Act.

2 Look and say.

Let's learn!

There **was** a park in our town fifty years ago.

There **wasn't** a shopping mall in our town fifty years ago.

There **were** some funny trains one hundred years ago.

There **weren't** any planes two hundred years ago.

We use these time words when we talk about the past:
yesterday, last week / year / Monday, (fifty years) ago, then

We use **lots of** or **some** with 'There were'.
We use **any** with 'There weren't'.

In Australia, there were lots of kangaroos.

Wow! Australia is beautiful.

Yes, but we like living here with you!

3 Read and circle.

1 There **was** / were a park in our town one hundred years ago.

2 There **was** / **were** trains one hundred years ago.

3 There **was** / **were** motorbikes ninety years ago.

4 There **was** / **were** planes fifty years ago.

5 There **was** / **were** a hotel in the town ten years ago.

6 There **was** / **were** lots of buses twenty years ago.

4 Write. | was   were   wasn't   weren't |

1 There __wasn't__ a singer at the party last Saturday.

2 There _____ eight children at the party.

3 There _____ any flowers in the room.

4 There _____ a CD player in the room.

5 There _____ lots of sandwiches at the party.

6 There _____ a TV in the room.

1 **Speaking** Look and say.

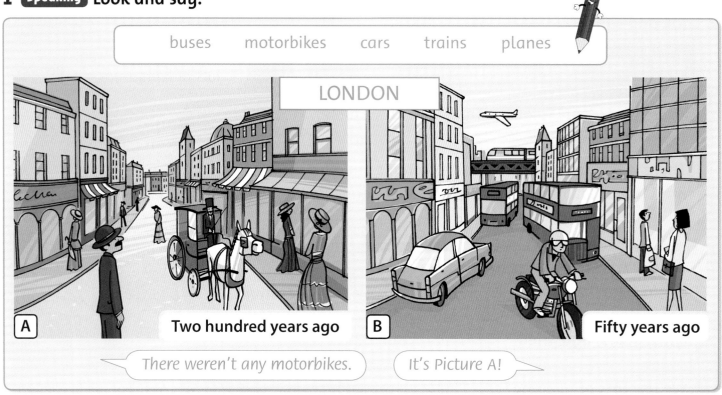

buses   motorbikes   cars   trains   planes

LONDON

A | Two hundred years ago

B | Fifty years ago

There weren't any motorbikes.   It's Picture A!

2 Write four sentences.

Two hundred years ago: There weren't any motorbikes. There ...

3 Listen and sing. 🎧 90

4 Sing and do.

Our town has a history

Our town has a history,
It's very old, you know!
Here's a picture of our town
Two hundred years ago.

There weren't any buses then,
And there weren't any trains.
There weren't any motorbikes,
And there weren't any planes.

There were shops and markets then,
And there were hotels, too.
There were parks and theatres,
There was a lot to do!

1 Listen, point and repeat. 91

ice cream   dream

queen   green

jelly   happy

2 Listen and chant. 92

In my dream,
I am a queen, queen, queen.
I eat green jelly,
With ice cream, cream, cream.
I'm very happy,
In my dream, dream, dream.

3 Read the chant again. Circle the words with *ea*, *ee* and *y*.

4 Write the words in the correct box.

tree   teacher   family   funny   week   sheep   eat   please   lolly

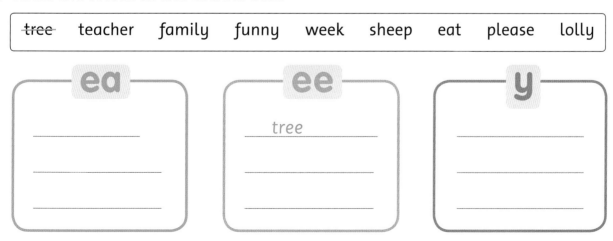

ea	ee	y
	tree	

Skills Time!

Reading

1 Listen, point and repeat. 🔊 93

 along
 through
 in the middle of
 at the top of
 between
 inside

2 Look at the text. Where is the Jorvik Viking Centre?

3 Listen and read. 🔊 94

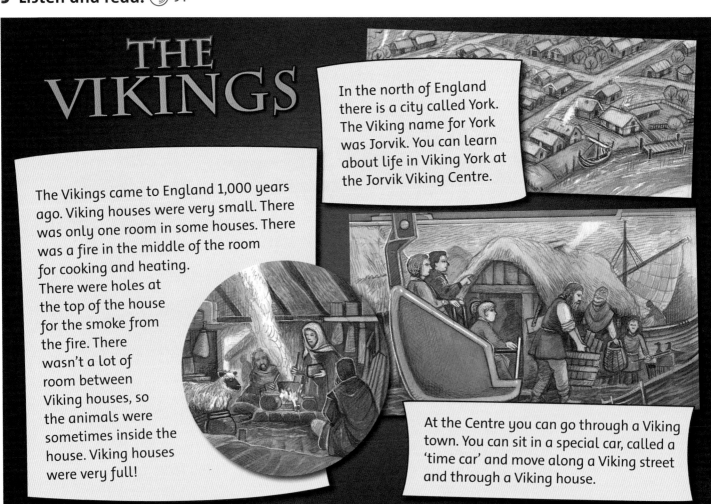

THE VIKINGS

In the north of England there is a city called York. The Viking name for York was Jorvik. You can learn about life in Viking York at the Jorvik Viking Centre.

The Vikings came to England 1,000 years ago. Viking houses were very small. There was only one room in some houses. There was a fire in the middle of the room for cooking and heating. There were holes at the top of the house for the smoke from the fire. There wasn't a lot of room between Viking houses, so the animals were sometimes inside the house. Viking houses were very full!

At the Centre you can go through a Viking town. You can sit in a special car, called a 'time car' and move along a Viking street and through a Viking house.

4 Read again and write.

| full | holes | fire | houses | room | ~~city~~ |

1 York is a _city_ in the north of England.　2 Viking houses were very ____ .

3 Viking ____ weren't big.　4 There was a ____ in the middle of the room

5 There was only one ____ in some houses.　6 There were ____ at the top of the house.

Listening

1 Listen and tick (✔) or cross (✗). 🔊 95

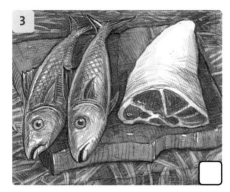

Speaking

2 Look at the pictures. Play the game.

| farmers | sheep | kitchens | chickens | cows | schools | meat | fish |

There were sheep in Viking times.   *It's Picture 5!*

Writing

We use paragraphs to make a text easier to read. We start a new paragraph for each separate topic in a text.

Paragraph 1 = Viking countries
There were Vikings in lots of countries a thousand years ago. There were Vikings in England, Russia and France. There were Vikings in America, too.

Paragraph 2 = Viking houses
There was only one room in most houses. There were bigger houses on farms. There was usually a living room, a kitchen and a bedroom in these houses.

3 Look at the text on page 78. How many paragraphs can you find?

12 A clever baby!

Lesson One Words

1 Listen, point and repeat. 96

old

young

handsome

pretty

short

tall

shy

friendly

2 Listen and read. 97

1
Holly	Look, Amy! We've got some old photos!
Max	This is Dad when he was young.
Dad	I'm still young!
Amy	Wow! He was handsome then!
Dad	I'm still handsome!

2
Holly	Look! This is Grandma when she was young.
Amy	Wow! Grandma was pretty!
Grandpa	I think Grandma is still pretty!

3
Max	Look at this photo of Grandpa!
Leo	Wow! He had black hair when he was young.
Grandpa	Yes, I've got white hair now.

4
Holly	And this photo is of Max when he was a baby!
Amy	Look! He had a book then, too!
Leo	He isn't different at all!

1 Listen to the story again and repeat. Act.

2 Look and say.

Let's learn!

> This is a photo of you when you were a baby.

I / He / She / It

He **was** handsome then.
I **wasn't** tall when I was five.

You / We / They

We **were** happy on holiday.
You **weren't** shy when you were six.

I / You / He / She / It / We / They

He **had** black hair when he was young.
You **didn't have** a book when you were a baby.

> Look! I had a bag then, too!

3 Read and circle.

1 They **were** / **weren't** at the park on Sunday.
2 It **was** / **wasn't** sunny.
3 The sea **was** / **wasn't** hot.
4 The children **were** / **weren't** hungry.
5 The baby **was** / **wasn't** happy.
6 The sandwiches **were** / **weren't** small.

Sunday

4 Write.   had   didn't have

They _had_ pizza for lunch last Friday.

The boys _____ a party last weekend.

He _____ a guitar lesson yesterday.

The girls _____ a picnic last Saturday.

1 **Speaking** **Look and say.**

long hair   short hair   short   tall   shy   friendly

2 years old

8 years old

She had long hair.   She was eight years old.

2 Write about Helen.

When she was two years old, Helen had short hair. She was short. She was …

3 Listen and sing. 🔊 98

4 Sing and do.

When my grandpa was a boy

When my grandpa was a boy,
He was a lot like me.
He had a house and garden,
And a happy family.

Grandpa was a happy boy,
And he had lots of friends.
They had lessons every day,
And they had fun at weekends.

When my grandpa was a boy,
He had fun every day.
He had lots of books to read,
And lots of games to play.

1 Listen, point and repeat. 🔘 99

2 Listen and chant. 🔘 100

In the dry, night sky
There's a light so white.
It makes me smile
As it shines all night.

3 Read the chant again. Circle the words with *igh*, *y* and *i_e*.

4 Match and write.

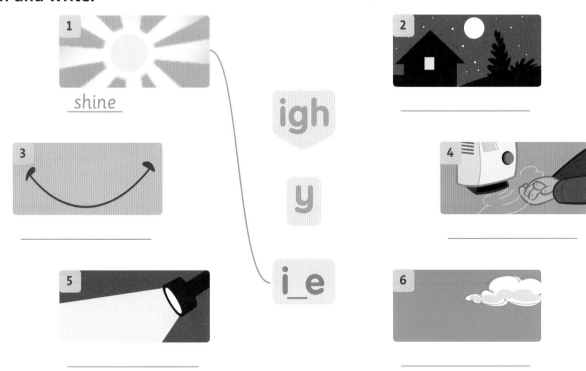

shine

igh

y

i_e

Skills Time!

Reading

1 Listen, point and repeat. 🔊 101

cheerful

miserable

relaxed

worried

mean

generous

2 Describe what you can see in the pictures below.

3 Listen and read. 🔊 102

My Grandma

When my grandma was a girl,
Her eyes were bright and blue.
She had lovely, long, black hair,
Her face was pretty, too.
In this photo I can see,
What grandma was like then.
Grandma was a lot like me,
When she was only ten.

Grandma had her wedding day,
When she was twenty-two.
She was a very pretty bride,
The groom was handsome, too.
That young groom's my grandpa now,
And I am very glad.
Next they had a baby boy,
That baby was my dad.

Now my grandma's seventy,
Her hair is short and grey.
She's very cheerful all the time,
She's happy every day.
She's always nice and generous,
I think that you can see,
I love my grandma very much,
And I know that she loves me.

4 Read again and write *T* (true) or *F* (false).

1 Grandma had short hair when
she was a girl. _F_

2 Grandma was pretty when
she was a girl. ___

3 Grandma is sixty now. ___

4 Grandma is sometimes miserable. ___

5 Grandma is never generous. ___

6 Grandma has grey hair now. ___

Listening

1 Listen and tick (✔). 🎧 103

Speaking

2 Look at the pictures. Play the game.

> blond hair / brown hair   a red bike / a blue bike
> a big house / a small house   cheerful / miserable

He had blond hair when he was a boy.

*False! He didn't have blond hair.
He had brown hair.*

Writing

We use **and** to link two positive ideas.
We use **but** to link a positive and
a negative idea.
We use a comma (**,**) before **but**.

Helen is happy **and** cheerful.
Tom is handsome, **but** he is miserable.

3 Write *and* or *but*.

1 My grandma is old, _but_ she is very
   pretty.
2 Susan is pretty, _____ she is mean.
3 Jack is miserable, _____ he is handsome.
4 You are kind _____ generous.

1 Complete the crossword.

Down

Across

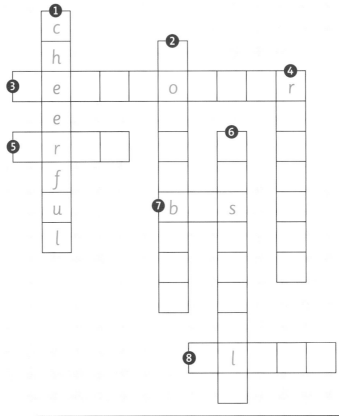

Crossword grid:

Down:
1 c h e e r f u l
2 o
4 r
5 r
6 s
7 b

Across:
3 (starts with e)
5
7 b ... s
8 l

2 Write the correct words.

litter   bin   path   grass   fountain   ~~trees~~

This is a nice park. There are two ¹ _trees_ in the park and
there are lots of flowers. A woman is standing near a
² _____. A boy is walking on the ³ _____ and a
girl is walking on the ⁴ _____. A man is cleaning the
park. He is taking all the ⁵ _____ and he is putting it
in the ⁶ _____. The park is very clean now.

3 Write.   must   mustn't

SCHOOL RULES

1 You _must_ do your homework.
2 You _____ shout in the classroom.
3 You _____ help your teacher.
4 You _____ use your mobile phone at school.
5 You _____ play football in the classroom.
6 You _____ put litter in the bin.

4 Write.

| was   were   wasn't   weren't |

This is a photo of our street fifty years ago. There
¹ _were_ houses in the street then. There ² _____
any trams. There ³ _____ cars and motorbikes.
There ⁴ _____ a shopping mall, but there ⁵ _____
two shops. There ⁶ _____ a cinema, too.

5 Write.

| had   didn't have |

1 Lisa _had_ short hair when she was a baby.
2 She _____ long hair.
3 She _____ a toy car.
4 She _____ a mobile phone.
5 She _____ a book.
6 She _____ a bike.

6 Read and complete the words.

| ai   ay   a_e |

All the drinks are on the
tr _a_ _y_ .

There is a lot of r___ ___n
today. We can't go outside.

I can run fast. I was the
winner in the r___ c___.

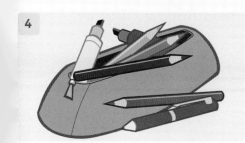

My pens and pencils are
in my pencil c___ s___ .

I play with my tr___ ___n.

Every Saturd___ ___ I visit
my grandma.

1 Look at the picture. What are the animals doing?

Toad's Motor Car

Toad loved motor cars, but he was a terrible driver. The stables at Toad Hall were full of broken motor cars. Toad's friends were worried about him. "He spends too much money on cars," said Rat. "He's been in hospital three times," said Mole. "It's time to teach him a lesson," said Badger.

The three animals went to Toad Hall. There was a shiny new motor car outside the house. Toad was getting ready for a drive. "You're just in time!" he said. Then he saw how serious his friends looked and he felt very worried. "Take him into the house," said Badger.

Toad shouted and kicked, but Rat and Mole carried him inside. "You have been very foolish, Toad," said Badger. "It's time we talked about motor cars." Badger took Toad into the library and closed the door. After a long time, the door opened again and a very sorry Toad appeared.

"Toad knows that he has been very foolish," said Badger. "He has promised never to drive a motor car again." "Oh, Toad," said Mole, happily. "Is that true?" Toad tried to look sad and serious, but he could not do it. "No!" he shouted. "I love motor cars! I only said I was sorry because I wanted you to let me out of the library!"

Badger was very angry. "Then we have no choice," he said. "We must take away your car keys. Now, I want you to go to your bedroom until you are sorry. When you promise to forget about motor cars, you can come out again." Toad went to his bedroom. He wasn't happy, but he didn't want to argue with Badger.

"Do you think Toad really will forget about motor cars?" asked Mole. "Maybe," said Rat. "But it will take a very long time." "I think you're right," said Badger. "But we are Toad's friends. We will wait."

2 Read and tick (✓) or cross (✗).

1 Toad is a good driver. ☐   2 Badger takes Toad into the library. ☐

3 Toad wants to go to his bedroom. ☐   4 Badger took Toad's car keys. ☐

3 Look at the picture. What kind of vehicle is this?

M-400 Skycar

Is this the car of the future? The developers of the M-400 Skycar certainly hope so. The M-400 Skycar is a flying car, but you don't need to be a pilot to fly it. It is easy to drive, because the controls are like the controls in a car. The car also has a computer to help the driver. The driver can tell the computer what direction they want to fly in and how fast they want to go and then the computer controls the car.

The car can hold four people, but there are plans for a single-seat and a six-seat version of the vehicle. The car is small enough to keep in a garage and will use the same amount of fuel as a large car. The car makes a lot of noise when it takes off, but the noise doesn't last for long, because the car climbs into the air very quickly. The car can fly at very high speeds and it can also move on the ground for short distances. At the moment, the car is very expensive. It costs about $1 million, but the developers are planning to use cheaper engines to make the car easier to afford. They want the car to be the same price as a normal large, comfortable car. But the best news is that the car uses ethanol and water instead of petrol, so it doesn't pollute the air. The developers expect the Skycar to be ready in 2012.

4 Read and write *T* (true) or *F* (false).

1 The Skycar can travel on land. ___

2 The Skycar uses petrol. ___

3 A computer controls the car. ___

4 The car can hold five people. ___

5 Ask and answer.

1 Do you think the Skycar is the car of the future?

2 What's your favourite way to travel?

Lesson One Words

1 Listen, point and repeat. 🔊 104

start

finish

love

hate

want

use

laugh

live

2 Listen and read. 🔊 105

1

Amy Look, Leo! It's some Ancient Egyptian writing.

Max It's our homework. It's a secret message from our teacher.

Amy But we can't read it.

Max We can look in my book!

2

Max The Ancient Egyptians lived 5,000 years ago. They used pictures, not words. This is their alphabet.

Amy The … Ancient … Egyptians … cooked … lots … of … nice food …

Max Bring … an … Ancient … Egyptian … dish … to … school!

Amy Ancient Egyptians cooked rice. Let's make that!

3

Amy It's ready! Let's play!

4

Amy Where is our dish?

Grandpa Oh! I'm sorry. I was hungry.

Max Grandpa! That was our homework!

1 Listen to the story again and repeat. Act.

2 Look and say.

Let's learn!

I / You / He / She / It / We / They

They **lived** 5,000 years ago.
They **didn't live** in flats.

didn't = did **not**

What's for dinner, Mum?

We've got fish pie for dinner, but Mum didn't cook it. I cooked it! It's ready! Let's eat!

3 Read and circle.

Ellie (finished) / **didn't finish** her homework last night.

Dad **started** / **didn't start** reading a book yesterday.

The children **loved** / **didn't love** the cake at the party.

He **hated** / **didn't hate** the dinner.

4 Write.

A very, very long time ago, people ¹ _didn't live_ (not live) in houses. They ² _____ (not cook) in kitchens. They ³ _____ (cook) on fires. They ⁴ _____ (not watch) television and they ⁵ _____ (not listen) to music. Men and women ⁶ _____ (work) and children ⁷ _____ (play) games.

1 [Speaking] **Look and say. Tick (✔) or cross (✗).**

watch television   cook   play the guitar
listen to music   play football

You	✔				
Your friend					

I listened to music yesterday.
I didn't watch TV yesterday. I …

2 Write four sentences about you.

I watched television yesterday. I didn't play football yesterday. I …

3 Listen and sing. 🎵 106

4 Sing and do.

My birthday!

It was my birthday yesterday!
I didn't shop or cook,
I opened lots of birthday cards
And started a good book.

It was my birthday yesterday!
My day was really great!
Lots of friends came round for tea,
We finished all the cake!

It was my birthday yesterday!
Hooray! Hooray! Hooray!
I had a party with my friends,
We sang and danced and played!

1 **Listen, point and repeat.**  107

snow   elbow   coat   soap   nose   stone

2 **Listen and chant.** 108

I put on my coat
And go out in the snow.
There is snow on my nose
And on my elbow.

3 Read the chant again. Circle the words with *ow*, *oa* and *o_e*.

4 Circle the odd-one-out.

1 snow   (soap)   show   slow   2 home   bone   snow   stone
3 soap   rope   coat   boat   4 boat   coat   goat   bone

5 Write the words in the correct box.

| show   home   boat   slow   coat   those   goat   bone   snow |

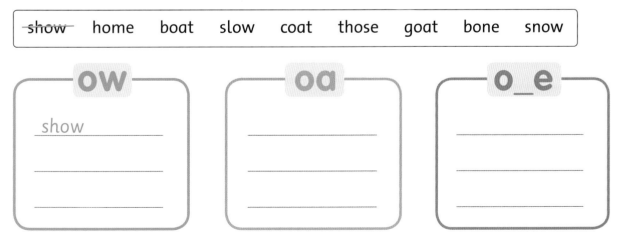

ow

show
_____

_____

_____

oa

_____

_____

_____

o_e

_____

_____

_____

Reading

1 Listen, point and repeat. 🔊 109

heavy

light

hard

soft

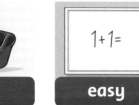

easy

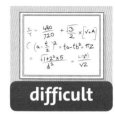

difficult

2 Look at the text below. Who wanted to make paper?

3 Listen and read. 🔊 110

Papyrus

Five thousand years ago, there was no paper. People used clay tablets to write on. They used a reed to write on the wet clay. Then they waited for the clay to dry. The tablets were very heavy. They were easy to break. People used each tablet only one time.

The Ancient Egyptians wanted to make paper to write on. Three thousand years ago, there were lots of papyrus plants in Egypt. The Ancient Egyptians used papyrus to make a kind of paper. It was difficult to make, but it was soft and light and easy to write on.

People in other countries started to use papyrus, too. But papyrus was very expensive. Only rich people used it. Sometimes people used the papyrus, then washed it and used it again.

Do you know?

The word 'paper' comes from the word 'papyrus'.

4 Read again and write.

~~heavy~~ light expensive soft easy difficult

1 Clay tablets were _heavy_ .

2 Clay tablets were _____ to break.

3 Papyrus was very _____ to make.

4 Papyrus wasn't heavy. It was _____ .

5 Papyrus was _____ . It was easy to write on.

6 Only rich people used papyrus. It was _____ .

Listening

1 Listen and write the numbers. 🔊 111

Speaking

2 Look at the pictures. Play the game.

> have difficult homework   have a maths lesson   play basketball
> have an English lesson   work for three hours   not know the answers
> start to rain   not have his homework

(The boy played basketball.)   (It's Picture A!)

Writing

Remember!
In each paragraph there is one topic.

3 Match the topics to the paragraphs.

a _Jobs_   The Ancient Egyptians lived in Egypt thousands of years ago. They had lots of different jobs. A lot of Ancient Egyptians were farmers, but there were teachers, artists and writers, too.

1 Houses

2 Children

b _____   They lived in small houses. The houses had kitchens, living rooms and bedrooms.

3 Jobs

c _____   The children worked with their parents and helped at home. Children in Ancient Egypt had toys and they played lots of games.

4 Food

d _____   The Ancient Egyptians cooked lots of good food. They cooked rice, bread, meat and fish.

Lesson One Words

1 Listen, point and repeat. 112

paint

paintbrush

calculator

lunch box

dictionary

PE kit

backpack

apron

2 Listen and read. 113

1

Mum Did you have a good day?
Amy No! First we had PE, but I didn't have my PE kit.

2

Amy Next, we had maths, but I didn't have my calculator.

3

Amy Then we had lunch, but I didn't have my lunch box.
Mum What did you eat?
Max Amy had some of my lunch.

4

Max Then we had art and Amy dropped her paint.
Amy The paint went onto my clothes!
Mum But you have an apron for art!
Amy My apron, my calculator and my PE kit were in my backpack and my backpack was at home.
Leo Amy didn't have her backpack! I don't believe it!

1 Listen to the story again and repeat. Act.

2 Look and say.

Let's learn!

I / You / He / She / It / We / They

Did you **have** a good day?
Yes, I **did.**   No, I **didn't.**

What did you watch last night?   A film.
Where did you watch the film?   At home.
When did the film finish?   At nine o'clock.

3 Read and circle.

1 (**What**) / **Where** did Jenny paint? A picture of her house.

2 **Where** / **When** did you visit your cousins? Last week.

3 **Where** / **What** did the boys have a picnic? In the park.

4 **What** / **When** did you have for dinner last night? Pizza.

5 **What** / **Where** did the girls play tennis? At the sports centre.

6 **Where** / **When** did the children have breakfast today? At seven o'clock.

4 Write.

Did he walk to school yesterday?

No, he didn't.

Did they have lunch at school today?

_____

Did she use a calculator?

_____

Did he have his PE kit today?

_____

1 (Speaking) **Ask and answer.**

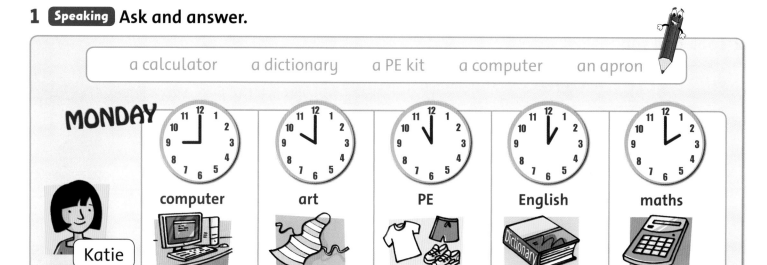

a calculator   a dictionary   a PE kit   a computer   an apron

| When did Katie have an English lesson? | At one o'clock. |
| What did Katie use in her English lesson? | Her dictionary. |

2 Write two questions and answers.

What did Katie use in her English lesson? A dictionary.

3 Listen and sing. 114

4 Sing and do.

Did you have a good day?

Did you have a good day at school today?
Did you paint a picture at school today?
Did you play a new game at school today?
Did you have lots of fun?

Did you like your lessons at school today?
Did you help your teacher at school today?
Did you have a good day at school today?
Did you have lots of fun?

1 Listen, point and repeat. 🔊 115

moon   boot   blue   glue   tune   tube

2 Listen and chant. 🔊 116

It's Tuesday night,
And I'm not at (school).
I've got glue and tubes,
And paint that's blue.

I make a toy flute,
I look up at the moon.
It's a hot June night,
And I play a tune.

3 Read the chant again. Circle the words with *oo*, *ue* and *u_e*.

4 Match and write.

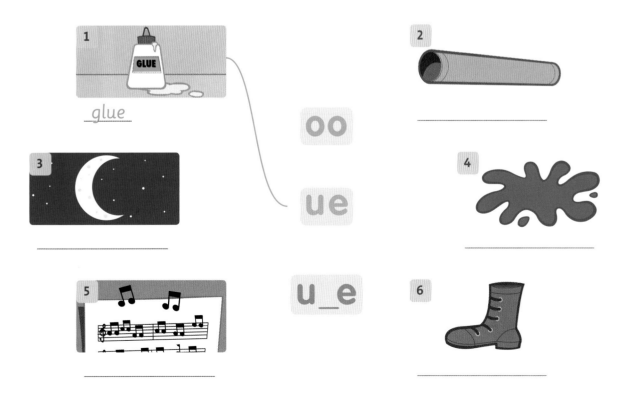

1 glue

2

oo

3

4

ue

5

u_e   6

Skills Time!

Reading

1 Listen, point and repeat. 🔊 117

tent

sleeping bag

frying pan

matches

rope

torch

2 Describe what you can see in the pictures below.

3 Listen and read. 🔊 118

School Camping Trip

Last month, twenty students from Year 8 were on the school camping trip. TOM WALTERS tells us all about it.

Where did you stay?
We stayed in tents near a river. It was fun!

Did you have lessons?
No, we didn't, but we fished every day and we learned how to make a bridge over the river, too. We used rope and wood.

Was it cold at night?
No, it wasn't. We had warm sleeping bags. It was very dark, but we had torches. One night, there was a noise outside. We were scared, but when we looked outside, there was only a cat.

What did you eat?
We cooked food in frying pans on a fire. Sometimes we cooked the fish from the river! One day it rained and our matches were wet. So we started a fire with two sticks!

4 Read again and answer the questions.

1 Did the children stay in tents? _Yes._

2 Did the children use rope to make a bridge? _____

3 Did the children stay near a beach? _____

4 Did the children cook in a kitchen? _____

5 Did the children have lessons? _____

6 Did it rain? _____

Listening

1 Listen and write the numbers. 🔊 119

Speaking

2 Look at the pictures. Ask and answer.

> have lessons   visit his grandma and grandpa
> stay in a tent   cook on a fire
> play volleyball   listen to CDs

Did the boy visit his grandma and grandpa last week?

No, he didn't.

Writing

Remember!

We use **time words** in stories or articles to show the order of events.

1 First   2 Then
3 Next   4 Finally

3 Number the sentences in the correct order.

Last Friday, I was on a school trip. We visited the zoo.

A ☐ Next, we had lunch in a café at the zoo.
B ☐ Finally, we painted pictures of our favourite animals.
C 1 First, we watched the monkeys and the elephants.
D ☐ Then, we looked at the penguins and the kangaroos.

15 Our holiday!

Lesson One   Words

1 Listen, point and repeat. 🔊 120

suitcase

sun cream

towel

soap

shampoo

hairbrush

toothbrush

toothpaste

2 Listen and read. 🔊 121

Amy I can't wait to start our holiday!
Dad Come on, Amy. Put your suitcase in the car.
Amy I'm not going to take a suitcase. I've got all my things in my backpack.
Mum Oh, Amy!

Dad Leo, your suitcase is very big. What have you got in it?
Leo My skateboard. I'm going to skateboard every day!
Mum Oh, Leo!

Max Can you help me with my suitcase, please?
Amy Oh! It's very heavy!
Max I know. Be careful!

Amy Look at all these books!
Max I'm going to read them on our holiday.
Mum Oh, Max. You haven't got any clothes in your suitcase. What are you going to wear?

1 Listen to the story again and repeat. Act.

2 Look and say.

Let's learn!

I

I'm **going to** skateboard every day.

Are you **going to** swim in the sea?
Yes, I **am**. No, I'm not.

He / She / It

He's **going to** play basketball tomorrow.

Is she **going to** visit her cousins tomorrow?
Yes, she **is**. No, she **isn't**.

We / You / They

We're **going to** have a great holiday.

Are they **going to** swim in the sea?
Yes, they **are**. No, they **aren't**.

I'm going to read my book.

Our holiday is going to be great! I'm going to swim in the sea.

We use these time words with *going to*: tomorrow, soon, later, next week / month / year

3 Read and circle.

1 We **is** / **are** going to go on holiday next week.

2 I **'m** / **'re** going to take my hairbrush on holiday.

3 Mum and Dad **am** / **are** going to buy soap and toothpaste tomorrow.

4 Jack **is** / **are** going to put sun cream on when he goes to the beach.

4 Write. | 'm 's 're |

She __'s__ going to make a cake.

They ___ going to watch a DVD.

I ___ going to wash the car.

It ___ going to rain.

Lesson Three Grammar and Song

1 **Speaking** **Ask and answer.**

a camera   some sun cream   a towel   a hat   some soap   some shampoo
a hairbrush   a swimsuit   a toothbrush   some toothpaste

Emma   Alex   Katie   Tom   Lucy   Billy

Is Emma going to take a camera?

Yes, she is. Is Tom going to take some sun cream?

No, he isn't. Is Katie going to take a hairbrush?

Yes, she is. Is …?

2 **Write about a boy or a girl.**

Alex is going to take a towel on holiday. He's …

3 **Listen and sing.** 122

4 **Sing and do.**

I'm going to pack my suitcase

I'm going to pack my suitcase,
I'm going to go away.
I'm going to have a great time,
I'm going on holiday!

I'm going to take some sun cream,
And also some shampoo.
I'm going to take my toothbrush,
And some toothpaste, too.

I'm going to take some photos,
I'm going to see the sea.
I'm going to swim and windsurf,
I'm going to waterski!

1 Listen, point and repeat. 🎧 123

book
wool

wood

hood
cook

2 Listen and chant. 🎧 124

It's a very cold day.
I've got a coat with a hood.
I've got my wool scarf,
And I'm feeling good.

I'm sitting on some wood.
I'm looking at my book.
The book's very good.
It tells me how to cook.

3 Read the chant again. Circle the words with *oo*.

4 Complete the words. Listen and check. 🎧 125

1

2

3

4

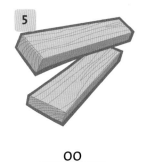
5

c oo k   __ oo __   __ oo __   __ oo __   __ oo __

5 Write a word that rhymes.

1

book _____

2

wood _____

Skills Time!

Reading

1 Listen, point and repeat. 🔊 126

| tomorrow | later | tonight | this afternoon | soon | next week |

2 Look at the text. Where is Lisa on holiday?

3 Listen and read. 🔊 127

Hi Ellie,

How are you? Are you having a nice holiday? I'm having a great time in Spain!

It's great weather here! It's very hot and sunny. My family and I go to the beach every day. The beach is a lot of fun because you can do lots of water sports here. I'm going to waterski this afternoon and my brother is going to windsurf.

The food here is great. We're going to eat in a seafood restaurant tonight. I love seafood. I want to try octopus!

We're going to visit a museum tomorrow morning. It is about the history of Spain. Then tomorrow afternoon we're going to go shopping in the town. We want to buy some presents. I want to get you a present from Spain.

We're going to fly home next week. I want to show you all my photos!

See you soon.

Best wishes,

Lisa

Ellie Harris,
4 Bluebell Lane,
Oxford,
OT2 9LM
England

4 Read again and write *T* (true) or *F* (false).

1 Lisa is in Australia. _F_

2 Lisa is going to waterski this afternoon. ___

3 Lisa's family are going to eat seafood tonight. ___

4 Lisa doesn't like seafood. ___

5 Lisa is going to buy Ellie a present. ___

6 Lisa is going to fly home tomorrow. ___

Listening

1 Listen and circle. 🔊 128

Harry's holiday

Monday	Tuesday	Wednesday	Thursday	Friday
visit the zoo	help my dad	watch TV	watch TV	ride my bike
play football	ride my bike	help my dad	visit the zoo	play football

Speaking

2 Ask and answer about you.

ride my bike	watch television	visit family	do my homework
help my mum	play football	listen to music	play with my friend
read a book	go to the park	write an email	have a music lesson

What are you going to do on Monday?

What are you going to do on Tuesday?

I'm going to watch television.

I'm going to do my homework.

Writing

We use these phrases to start and end an email or letter.

Start	End
Dear ...	Write soon.
Hi ...	See you soon.
How are you?	Bye for now.
Thanks for your email.	Take care.
	Best wishes,

Check that your email or letter has clear paragraphs and correct punctuation before you send it.

3 Write S for comments at the Start or E for comments at the End.

1 Write soon. [E]

2 Dear Amy, [ ]

3 Thanks for your email. [ ]

4 How are you? [ ]

5 Hi Ben, [ ]

6 Take care. [ ]

1 Complete the crossword.

Down

Across

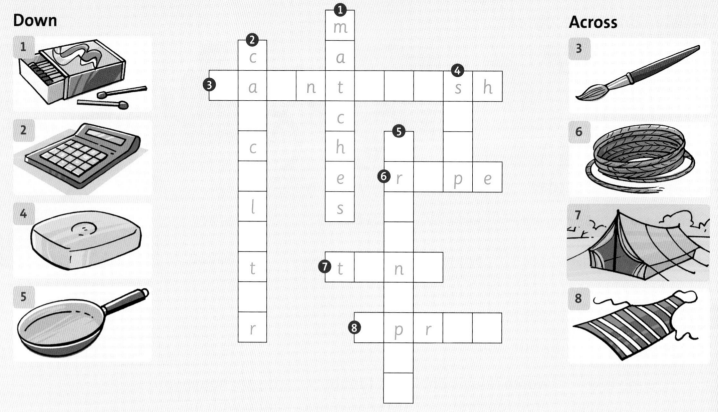

2 Write the correct words.

| toothbrush | sun cream | towel | shampoo | hairbrush | ~~suitcase~~ |

Emma is going to Italy on holiday. She's putting all her things in her ¹ _suitcase_ now. She's going to take her ² _____ to use after swimming. She's going to take her ³ _____ to brush her teeth. She's going to take some ⁴ _____ to wash her hair and she's going to take a ⁵ _____ to brush her hair. She's going to take some ⁶ _____ because the sun is very hot in Italy.

3 Read and circle.

1 Mum **listened** / **didn't listen** to music yesterday.

2 The girl **played** / **didn't play** a game.

3 Dad **cooked** / **didn't cook** dinner.

4 The boys **played** / **didn't play** a game.

5 Mum **watched** / **didn't watch** TV.

6 The girls **listened** / **didn't listen** to music.

Yesterday

4 Write the answers.

Last Saturday

1 Did the family stay in the house last Saturday?
   No, they didn't.
2 Did Mum work in the garden? _____
3 Did the girls have a picnic? _____
4 Did Dad wash the car? _____
5 Did it rain? _____
6 Did the boys play volleyball? _____

5 Write. | 'm   's   're |

My family and I are very happy. We ¹ _'re_ going to visit
our cousins next week. Our cousins live near the beach, so
they ² _____ going to take us to the beach every day.
I ³ _____ going to swim in the sea. My brother doesn't
like swimming. He ⁴ _____ going to play volleyball on the
beach. Mum is happy because she ⁵ _____ going to read
her new book. We ⁶ _____ going to have a great holiday.

6 Read and complete the words. | ue   u_e   oo |

1
I like my new teacher at
sch_o__o_l.

2
Can you play a t__n__ on
the guitar?

3
How many r_____ms are
in your flat?

4
My favourite colour is
bl_____ .

5
At night I can see stars and the
m_____n.

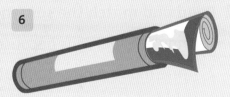

6
There is a big poster in
the t__b___ .

Extensive reading: School

1 Look at the picture. How do you think the people feel?

The first day of school

Anne felt nervous as she entered the classroom. Just last year, she was a student and now she was a teacher. It was strange to be on the other side of the teacher's desk.

The children were ready for lessons to begin. Anne had a speech to give the children about helping and learning, but now she could not remember one word of it.

"Please take your books out," she said. While the children opened their desks and took out their books, Anne looked at them all. Most of the children looked cheerful, but a few seemed unfriendly.

The day passed quickly. Later, Anne couldn't remember it very well. It was like a dream. She listened to the children read, she helped them with sums and she set them exercises. Only two of the children were naughty. The first was Morley Andrews. He took out his two pet grasshoppers during the lesson. The second was Anthony Pye. He poured a few drops of water down Aurelia Clay's neck. Anne made Morley stand at the front of the class for an hour and she kept Anthony in at break to talk to him about good manners.

At the end of the day, the children left and Anne packed up her things. She felt tired and a little bit sad. She didn't know if she liked teaching after all. She locked the school door and started to walk home. At the bottom of the hill she met one of the boys from her class. He gave her a small bunch of wild flowers.

"I came back to give you these," he said. "I thought you might like them. And I like you, teacher." Anne took the flowers and smiled. "Thank you," she said. "They're beautiful." Suddenly Anne didn't feel tired at all. She was happy and hopeful.

2 Read and match the sentence halves.

1 Anne was nervous because ☐

2 Anne made a boy stand at the front because ☐

3 Anne was a little bit sad because ☐

a he took out his pet grasshoppers during the lesson.

b it was her first day as a teacher.

c she didn't know if she liked teaching.

3 Look at the pictures. What school event do the pictures show?

Sports day

My name's Emma and I'm from Britain. My favourite day in the school year is Sports Day. Sports Day in Britain is lots of fun. Schools usually have Sports Day in the summer, near the end of the school year, because the weather is warm and sunny then. Children run races and try to win prizes or trophies. There is often a skipping race, a sack race (children stand in a sack and jump along the race track), or a three-legged race (children run in pairs, with the left leg of one runner strapped to the right leg of the other runner). Children's parents come to watch Sports Day. Sometimes there are races for mums and dads, too. Everyone has a great time.

Hi. I'm Takumi. I love Sports Day, too. In Japan, we have Sports Day in the autumn or spring, because the weather is cooler then. It's too hot to run races in the summer in Japan. We don't have any lessons for a week before Sports Day. We practise our races and events on the school field every day. The teachers always make sure that we drink lots of water, because we get hot from all the exercise. There is a big rehearsal on the day before Sports Day, to make sure that everything will go well on the actual day. We usually have Sports Day on a Sunday. The school band plays music and we all run races and take part in competitions. It's a wonderful day and we all enjoy it.

4 Read and answer the questions.

1 Why do Japanese schools have Sports Days in autumn?

2 Why do British schools have Sports Days in summer?

3 What do Japanese children do the week before the Sports Day?

4 Do you have Sports Day at your school?

5 Who is your favourite teacher? Why?

1 Look at the picture. What are the boys doing?

The Prince and the Pauper

Tom Canty was a boy from a very poor family. His clothes were old and dirty and he never had enough food. However, Tom believed that he could have a better life one day. He was clever and he knew how to read and write. He wanted to get a good job and earn enough money to have a house, clothes and good food.

One day, Tom was outside the palace gates when he saw Prince Edward. Tom stood and watched the Prince for a while. The guards tried to send Tom away, but the Prince stopped them. The two boys were very surprised when they saw each other. They had very different lives, but they looked just the same. They had the same eyes, the same hair and the same faces. The only thing that was different was their clothes. Prince Edward invited Tom into the palace and the two boys talked about their lives. Edward had lots of money, fine clothes, jewels and plenty of food, but he had to stay in the palace and be quiet and good all the time. Tom had nothing, but he could play in the street with other boys and meet lots of interesting people.

"I want to be like you," Tom said to Edward. "You are rich and you can have everything you want." "I want to be like you," Edward said to Tom. "You are free and you can do everything you want." "Well, you look just like me, and we are the same age," said Edward. "Let's swap clothes. You can stay here and I can live with your family for a while." Tom thought this was a wonderful idea. The two boys swapped clothes and looked at each other.

"We are like twins," Tom laughed. Before Edward left the palace, he hid a wax disc in a suit of armour. Then he left the palace quickly, before the guards found the two boys together. Soon Edward was with Tom's family, but it was not much fun. Tom's father was unkind. He was often angry and he shouted at Edward all the time. Edward wanted to leave. He ran away and met a soldier called Miles Hendon.

2 Read and write short answers.

1 Was Tom Canty from a rich family? _____   2 Was Tom clever? _____

3 Did Edward want to be like Tom? _____   4 Was Tom's father kind? _____

5 Did Edward like life outside the palace? _____   6 Did Tom become King? _____

3 Ask and answer.

1 Who do you think has a better life: Edward or Tom? Why?

2 Why do you think the boys wanted to swap places?

3 Do you want to swap places with anyone? Who and why?

He was a kind man and he looked after Edward. They had lots of adventures together. Edward didn't really like life outside the palace. He saw that life was very difficult for poor people. He decided to be a good king and help the people of England.

Meanwhile, Tom was pretending to be the Prince. It wasn't easy. He didn't know how to act, or what to say to people. At first, people thought the Prince was ill, because he seemed so different. But Tom was a clever boy and he learned quickly. He had lots of good ideas and he was good at making important decisions. Soon everyone was sure that the Prince was well again.

Sadly, the King died while Edward was away. Prince Edward was now the King of England. Tom was very worried. He didn't want to be King. Luckily, Edward heard the news and came back to the palace. He arrived just in time. Tom was about to become the King of England. Edward and Tom tried to tell people the truth.

"I'm not Prince Edward," said Tom. "I'm Tom Canty."

"I'm the real Prince," said Edward. "We're sorry we lied. It was only a game."

Edward looked poor and dirty and people didn't believe that he was the real Prince. But Edward took the wax disc from the suit of armour and showed it to everyone. The wax disc was the Great Seal of England. Only the true King of England has the Great Seal. So Edward became King, but he remembered his adventures and the lessons he learned when he was with Miles. He was a good king and he helped the people of England. He made sure that life was better for poor people and Tom became a very important man. He was never poor or hungry again.

OXFORD
UNIVERSITY PRESS

Great Clarendon Street, Oxford OX2 6DP

Oxford University Press is a department of the University of Oxford.
It furthers the University's objective of excellence in research, scholarship,
and education by publishing worldwide in

Oxford New York

Auckland Cape Town Dar es Salaam Hong Kong Karachi
Kuala Lumpur Madrid Melbourne Mexico City Nairobi
New Delhi Shanghai Taipei Toronto

With offices in

Argentina Austria Brazil Chile Czech Republic France Greece
Guatemala Hungary Italy Japan Poland Portugal Singapore
South Korea Switzerland Thailand Turkey Ukraine Vietnam

OXFORD and OXFORD ENGLISH are registered trade marks of
Oxford University Press in the UK and in certain other countries

ISBN: 978 0 19 481224 5   Class Book
ISBN: 978 0 19 481231 3   Class Book and MultiROM pack
ISBN: 978 0 19 481234 4   MultiROM

Printed in China

This book is printed on paper from certified and well-managed sources.

ACKNOWLEDGEMENTS

Illustrations by: Adrian Barclay/Beehive Illustration pp 5, 9 (Ex3), 10 (Ex1), 15
(Ex3, 4), 16 (Ex1), 21 (Ex3 & 4), 22 (Ex1), 26 (Ex1, 3), 27 (Ex4, 5), 30 (Ex3 & 4),
32 (Ex1), 37 (Ex3, 4), 38 (Ex1), 43 (Ex4), 44 (Ex1), 48 (Ex1, 2, 3), 49 (Ex5), 53
(Ex3), 54 (Ex1), 59 (Ex4), 60 (Ex1), 65 (Ex3), 70 (Ex1, 2), 71 (Ex4, 5), 75 (Ex3,
4), 76 (Ex1), 81 (Ex4), 82 (Ex1), 87 (Ex3, 4), 88 (Ex1), 92 (Ex1, 2), 93 (Ex4, 5),
97 (Ex3, 4), 98 (Ex1), 103 (Ex4), 104 (Ex1), 109 (Ex4), 110 (Ex1, 3), 114 (Ex1, 3),
115 (Ex4, 5); Kathy Baxendale pp 24 (Ex3), 25, 62 (Ex3), 63, 90 (Ex3), 91; Jared
Beckstrand pp 6, 10 (Ex3), 16 (Ex3), 22 (Ex3), 32 (Ex3), 38 (Ex3), 44 (Ex3), 54
(Ex3), 60 (Ex3), 66, 76 (Ex3), 82 (Ex3), 88 (Ex3), 98 (Ex3), 104 (Ex3), 110 (Ex3);
Seb Camajavec/Beehive Illustration pp 28, 116; Simon Clare pp 11, 17, 23,
27 (Ex6), 33, 39, 45, 49 (Ex6), 55, 61, 67, 71 (Ex6), 77, 83, 89, 93 (Ex6), 99, 105,
111, 115 (Ex6); Livia Coloji/The Organisation pp 94, 118, 119; Steve Cox pp 12
(Ex3), 13, 78 (Ex3), 79; James Elston pp 4, 8 (Ex2), 9 (Ex2), 14 (Ex2), 15 (Ex2),
20 (Ex2), 21 (Ex2), 28 (Ex2), 29 (Ex2), 36 (Ex2), 37 (Ex2), 42 (Ex2), 43 (Ex2), 52
(Ex2), 53 (Ex1), 58 (Ex2), 59 (Ex1), 64 (Ex2), 65 (Ex2), 74 (Ex2), 75 (Ex2), 80
(Ex2), 71 (Ex2), 86 (Ex2), 87 (Ex2), 96 (Ex2), 97 (Ex2), 102 (Ex2), 103 (Ex2), 108
(Ex2), 109 (Ex2); Paul Gibbs pp 40 (Ex3), 41, 56 (Ex3), 57; Andrew Hennessey
pp 7, 8 (Ex1), 12 (Ex1), 14 (Ex1), 18 (Ex1), 20 (Ex1), 24 (Ex1), 26 (Review
banner), 27 (Review banner), 30 (Ex1), 34 (Ex1), 36 (Ex1), 40 (Ex1), 42 (Ex1),
48 (Review banner), 49 (Review banner), 52 (Ex1), 56 (Ex1), 58 (Ex1), 62 (Ex1),
64 (Ex1), 68 (Ex1), 70 (Review banner), 71 (Review banner), 74 (Ex1), 78 (Ex1),
80 (Ex1), 84 (Ex1), 86 (Ex1), 90 (Ex1), 92 (Review banner), 93 (Review banner),
96 (Ex1), 100 (Ex1), 102 (Ex1), 106 (Ex1), 108 (Ex1), 115 (Review banner), 115
(Review banner); Brian Lee pp 84 (Ex3), 85; Carl Pearce/Advocate pp 35, 112,
113; Jorge Santillan/Beehive Illustration p 50; Harris Sofoleous/ Sylvie Poggio
Artists Agency p 72.

Commissioned photography by: David Jordan pp 46, (Ellie head and shoulders), 47, 107.

With many thanks to the following locations: pp 107, Youlbury International Scout
Camp, Boars Hill, Oxford.

*The Publishers would like to thank the following for their kind permission to reproduce
photographs and other copyright material*: Alamy pp 18 (© Huw Jones/boy with
guitar), 19 (© People White Background/Ivan, © Imagebroker/Mai, © Helene
Rogers/Bruno, © Vario Images GmbH & Co.KG/boots and ball), Alamy pp 29
(© MIXA/girl, © Tetra/boy), 73 (© foodfolio/dolmades), 100 (© North Wind
Picture Archives/fragment of Book of The Dead), 106 (© Imagebroker/
food on campfire); Corbis p 19 (© Somos Images/Tina); Getty Images pp 18
(Taxi/Barbara Peacock/girls, Allsport Concepts/Pascal Rondeau/football),
19 (Taxi/DCA Productions/Billy, Photographer's Choice/Lauren Burke/
Shani), 34 (Photographer's Choice/Nancy Brown/girl with dolphin),68
(Gallo Images/Travel Ink/Mnajdra temples), 106 (Taxi/Titus Lacoste/fishing);
Getty Images p 117 (Taxi/ Nick Clements/sack race, Absodels/Japanese
girl); Jupiter Images pp 19 (Image Source/ingredients, Comstock Images/
fishing equipment); Masterfile p 26 (Peter Griffith/family); Masterfile p
73 (Michael Mahovlich/ceviche); OUP pp 19 (chess, Ting, Lisa), 68 (Russia
map); Photolibrary.com pp 34 (Pacific Stock/Wu Norbert/dolphins), 48
(Photolibrary/Richard Woldendorp/outback), 68 (Phototake Science/Tom
Carroll/Lake Pontchartrain Causeway), 112 (age fotostock/Javier Larrea); Rex
Features pp 51 (Action Press), 95; Science Photo Library p 68 (© NASA/The
Nile from space), 100 (Jack Coulthard/papyrus); Superstock p 106 (© Stock
Image/children around campfire).

Cover illustration by: James Elston